C A T H E R I N E
W A L K E R

CATHERINE
WALKER

HarperCollins*Publishers*

cover

AUTUMN/WINTER
COLLECTION 1989/90

Pink and white Buche silk crepe tailored dress.

HRH The Princess of Wales at the Royal Charity Performance of Swan Lake at the London Coliseum in Aid of the Royal Society for the Protection of Birds, November 1989.

The gala was in support of the rare Russian Bewick swans that migrate to Great Britain during the winter. This dress was chosen from the collection. The original design had a plunging V-neckline to a high waist but for this event the Princess felt this was a little indiscreet, so I decided to add an insert.

In a Vogue *article that autumn that featured this dress, Liz Tilberis commented through her editor Sarah Mower ". . . it is true to say that the praise that has been heaped upon the Princess of Wales's appearances recently has been due largely to the clothes Catherine Walker has designed for her. Fashion journalists have noted the evolution of a new way of dressing that has presence and dignity that is never overstated, middle-aged, or dowdy—an easy-seeming solution to the problematic question of how to dress a modern and attractive young woman who must nevertheless carry the weight of tradition and Royal expectation upon her shoulders. The achievement is that the Princess looks so at ease in Catherine's clothes."*

Photographer: Tim Graham

page ii

SPRING/SUMMER COLLECTION 1997

In my studio in a red Agnona single-breasted, knee-length blazer with my favourite tailor's stand. This stand was cast on a real person—tall, rounded shoulders, a slightly hollow chest, small bust, long midriff, and narrow hips. If a stand can be said to be inspiring, this one is.

Photographer: Geoff Wilkinson

First published in the United Kingdom in 1998
by HarperCollins*Publishers*

First published in the United States of America in 1998
by UNIVERSE PUBLISHING

A CIP catalogue record for this book is available from the British Library.

ISBN 000 414055 9

Design by Joel Avirom

Printed in England

Foreword

By Liz Tilberis

My first contact with Catherine Walker came about when I was a fashion editor at British *Vogue* in the mid-1980s. As an editor who wanted to represent British fashion in the magazine, I quickly cottoned onto the fact that if I had a story planned—say on a color theme, or using Prince of Wales check—Catherine would make me up something and we could shoot it for our pages. During that time, when Anna Wintour was editing the magazine, I remember a breakthrough moment: after years of working with a favorite model, Yasmin le Bon, and a favorite designer—Catherine—I finally managed to get them both on the cover. Yasmin was wearing a red Catherine Walker jacket—though I say it myself, it was a quintessentially eighties image, and even now the memory of what it meant to me hasn't faded.

Catherine and I became much closer when I was made editor of *Vogue* in 1987. Basically, she saved me. Here I was, not a size four but a size fourteen, with a wardrobe that mostly contained comfortable clothes that stylists wear on shoots—and virtually nothing in which I could look the part of the editor of British *Vogue*. Catherine rescued me, as she had rescued so many other British women with a semi-public role. Her clothes filled a void in London: she was exactly the person to go to if you wanted to have a perfect suit made or a beautiful evening dress. No wonder her star rose so brightly during those image-conscious times.

I'd go to her shop on Sydney Street, up the stairs to her workroom, and we'd talk about what I wanted and what she thought I should wear. The relief for me was Catherine's gentle combination of talents: the fact that she understood both fashion and a woman's psyche. She'd guide you into choices, never impose them on you. Although she has strong opinions on fashion, Catherine would never force a client into anything that made her feel uncomfortable—in either sense of the word. I loved my suits and my evening things from Catherine. One of my favorite pieces was a fabulous silver beaded jacket she made me for a party I hosted to celebrate the seventy-fifth anniversary of *Vogue*: I have it and treasure it still.

Most of all, Catherine's greatest gift to me was confidence—the confidence to wear fashionable clothes and feel like myself in them. Added to that, Catherine Walker is one of the most fiercely discreet people to walk the earth. I also suspect that both of those qualities—her confidence-enhancing design and her incredible loyalty—are what made for such a long and happy relationship between Catherine and the Princess of Wales. In the world of fashion, that combination is a rare thing indeed. For those reasons, reading this book is a moving experience for me. I'm glad that Catherine, who has effaced herself so much for the sake of her work and her clients, had finally given herself space to speak.

Preface

Sunday, 7 September 1997

By a strange quirk of fate this book was completed late on Saturday, 30 August, just hours before the shocking death of Diana, Princess of Wales. Sadly, I have had to change some of its contents. Diana and I had worked on the text and pictures together and on her last visit on Wednesday, 20 August, she quite casually said over a cup of coffee, "Would you like me to write the foreword?" It was a lovely surprise. I was very touched and gave her a kiss. However, I made a deal with her that she would have to read the finished text first, and she laughingly agreed. I was going to show it to her last Tuesday, 2 September, on her return from France. Of course I very much wanted Diana to write the foreword of my book but I would never have asked, and she knew it. I will cherish this memory.

The tables have turned, and now it is I who pay tribute to my friend.

Diana, Princess of Wales, was a very real woman in a unique situation. There was no precedent that she could look to for guidance. She had family and friends who loved her dearly, but ultimately nobody could tell her what to do or how to do it.

She was lonely at times, but she turned her fears and vulnerability into beauty and love and made so many people happy. She had the guts to remain true to herself—she walked tall with true spirit and style. I am immensely proud to have worked with her for all those years but mainly I feel very privileged to have known her as a real person. It is the idiosyncrasies of our friends that make them thankfully less perfect but so much more lovable, and she was very lovable. I will miss her so.

Catherine Walker

Introduction

A palmist once read my hand and told me that my life was split into two parts. "See," she said, pointing to the twin track lines that run around the base of my thumb, "One life ends here, and here another begins." I don't know if I believe in palmistry but on 27 August 1975 my life was jerked from one set of tracks and dumped onto another, for which it would be an understatement to say I was totally unprepared.

That day, my husband, John, who was thirty-two, and I were staying in the pretty hamlet of Buno Bonnevaux about sixty kilometres south of Paris near Fontainebleau. We had been invited by my cousin, Nico, and her husband, Pol, who owned a small farmhouse on the outskirts of the village. It was a hot summer and I had been ill, so John and I were glad to get away from London and enjoy the French countryside with our baby daughter, Marianne.

The previous night we had sent our elder daughter, Naomi, off for a few days with my mother to the Alps, and as her train pulled out of the station John was carrying Marianne on

John with our daughters: Naomi, aged two years, and Marianne, aged eight months.

his shoulders. I can still remember the expression of delight on her face when John said "And who's got Maman and Papa all to herself now?"

I had a strange feeling about John that day because for the first time since I had known him he had had a *siesta* after lunch. It may not have seemed odd to anyone else, but I also thought it was peculiar that he wore black and blue together, which I had never seen him do before. In fact, looking back on it, the preceding couple of weeks were full of omens and premonitions, or so it seemed.

After a game of tennis and a relaxed and very enjoyable dinner party we retired to our bedroom, where Marianne was asleep in a cot. During the night I told John how much better I was feeling. A few minutes later I got up to use the bathroom and was surprised to get a mild electric shock from the brass bedside lamp. I made my way to the bathroom on the other side of the hall.

I next remember a piercing shout and a loud thud. I ran to the bedroom but I could not open the door. I called Pol and Nico, and we forced open another door to the room. John was slumped against the first door, the bedside lamp lying on the tiled floor beside him. Although I tried what little first aid I knew to bring him back to life it was no use. He was dead.

In the ensuing seconds my body went numb and my mind empty and still. I automatically grabbed Marianne from her cot. No one knew what to do with us except to push us away as far as possible from the bedroom. I did what I was told and stood transfixed outside in the grounds next to a little lake, rocking Marianne in my arms. I watched the ambulance take John away. I wish I had stayed with him. I never even said good-bye.

Childhood

I was born on Friday, 27 June 1945, in Pont de Briques, a one-street village near Boulogne. The house where my mother gave birth to me was called "Neptune" after my father's long family history with the sea. The house had once been the grandest in the village, but by 1945 it was no longer so grand. In fact it was partly in ruins due to the events of the preceding five years—events that had started to shape my childhood even before I was born.

My parents moved into Neptune in 1939 after an elaborate wedding in Boulogne. There was a beautiful reception held at the house with a small orchestra playing Glen Miller music. Their happiness was rejoiced by the whole village but their marital bliss was short-lived, for within a few months the German army invaded northern France having

My parents' wedding day, July 1939.

outflanked the Maginot Line with little resistance. My father joined the French army as an officer of the *Artillerie*, but he was captured at Dunkirk and became a prisoner of war.

In Pont de Briques my mother recalls the arrival of the Germans. She was walking with friends along the beach on a bright morning in May 1940, pushing my newborn sister, Nicole, in her pram. Her attention was drawn to a humming sound along the beach which, as it grew nearer, turned out to be a small group of German infantry arriving on beige and dark green motorcycles. Within a few days they had requisitioned Neptune, the largest and most central building in Pont de Briques, and had it converted for use as an officer's mess.

This was a time of simply surviving for my mother. Food supplies were short, and there were no luxuries whatsoever. In fact, the Germans used to enter people's houses in Pont de Briques in the middle of the night to see if any luxuries were hidden or if radios were being used. Some said the French *gendarmerie* were worse than the Germans because they did the same but, being locals, they knew which luxuries were likely to be hidden and they confiscated them for their own use. My mother abandoned her house to the Germans and went to live on her sister-in-law's picturesque farm at Hem. However, even this proved intolerable as the Allies had started intensive bombing in the North. She fled to relatives in Tours and later to her relatives in Provence, which was in unoccupied France.

After the Normandy invasion the Germans in Pont de Briques left within twenty-four hours. Locals took the batteries from their cars because they knew the Germans were going to use every form of transport they could find. When my mother returned home in 1944, she was astonished to see the damage. The retreating German army had left Pas de Calais as a wasteland. All telephone wires were cut and the roads between Calais and Boulogne were virtually impassable even for those who could find petrol. This could be found a few miles north in Belgium, but it was illegal for the French to buy petrol, and the authorities had dyed it pink so that it could be detected.

It seemed that the Belgians had pulled themselves together with greater efficiency after the war than the French. They had traded with U.S. servicemen, and many more commodities were available over the border. There was even a tram service that passed between Lille and the border which was called "The Coffee Tram." Food was strictly rationed and although Pont de Briques had a *boulangerie* and *epicerie*, there were still no oranges, butter, or imported "luxuries" that are taken for granted today. Throughout the war (and for some time after), ladies painted "stockings" on their legs and edged them in pencil, but whatever the occasion all ladies wore hats and gloves.

My father had had a good wine cellar before the war and although he had bricked up the best vintages in one corner of the cellar and hidden the rest, it was all gone when he returned home. However, while having dinner with the local doctor two years after the war, he was struck by the familiar quality of the doctor's Gevrey-Chambertin. "You've stolen my wine," he declared with astonishment. "Yes, but it was either me or the Germans—which would you have preferred?" retorted the doctor. I think that is the pragmatic French way of seeing things. However

My mother in 1945 with my brother, Patrick, my sister, Nicole, and me, aged two weeks, on my christening day.

pragmatic or not, someone (or ones) in the village had a guilty conscience because for months after the war my father would receive little packets of lost belongings from anonymous senders.

When I was born in June 1945, Dr. Croqueloit, who delivered me, had to travel by tram from Boulogne and arrived several hours early having anticipated delays along the bombed and damaged Boulogne–Calais Road. Immediately after I was born my parents moved away from Pont de Briques and the memories of occupation in order to attempt a fresh start in neighbouring St. Leonard. But despite this new start and the arrival of both myself and my brother Patrick, the damage of the years of separation and the harshness and deprivations of the

At the farmhouse at Hem, aged four, with the family cat, Leo (Leopold).

war proved too much for the young couple. They divorced soon after, in 1949, when I was four. My father immediately married my mother's best friend, who had been the wife of his cousin and business partner. My mother was of course badly hurt. My parents refused to acknowledge each other thereafter and it was not until my wedding day twenty years later that I saw them together again.

After the divorce my father went to live in Port-en-Bessin in Normandy. As a result of family feuding he lost his share in his business, which was unfortunate for the business was substantial. It was started by his father and two of my uncles who, at the turn of the century, founded the first French company to manufacture boats with metal hulls. It was called *Fonderie et Atelier des Pompes et Moteurs* and employed eight hundred peo-

ple in the Port of Boulogne. My mother also suffered from this loss. With little financial support, she was obliged to move to the house of her own mother in Lille.

This residence resembled a double-fronted townhouse and was furnished with beautiful Provençale antiques. Everything was very formal. My grandparents would address each other as "vous" and there were cooks and maids who kept the upper wooden floors impeccably polished and the black-and-white stone tiles on the ground spotlessly clean.

Here we spent the next year with our doting grandparents. Each day my grandmother would feed me a spoonful of sticky syrup and some fat buttery biscuits. I was generally viewed as a frail child and indeed I nearly died of diphtheria at the age of eighteen months.

My grandfather was a great Bizet fan and would play old records of Carmen on a wind-up gramophone. He was quite Victorian in outlook and had a great respect for women, children, and the family. Until the day he died at age eighty-six he would walk three kilometres each day to his steel foundry, which he had started as a young man. Each day after school he would sit me on his knee and tell me old-fashioned children's stories, but if they became boring I used to pull his bow tie which took him several minutes to retie. He didn't mind and was always a little "too" slow to catch me untying it. Even at my young age I was aware that we had a very special relationship. The last words he uttered before he died were "Que Catherine marie un homme intelligent" (May Catherine marry an intelligent man).

At the time I was attending an elementary school in Lille. It was run by some nuns of the order Les Dames de St. Maur. My memory of this school still makes me shudder. The floors were of dark polished wood dimly lit through arched stained-glass windows. In this dimness the grim nuns, looking like fearsome *corbeaux* in their black habits, spoke in hushed tones as if a crime had just been committed. Even games were conducted in an atmosphere of impending punishment. It was here for the first time that I felt the stigma of my parents' divorce when one nun told me my divorced parents would be punished in hell for eternity. I think I cried for about two weeks, and I never forgot her sinister condemnation. My mother was my whole world, and I am sure I was not the first little child who wished their father had never existed.

Later on that year my mother decided it was time to move on. She had an idea that the best place for children to grow up was in the clear healthy air of the Alps. With this in mind she rented a house in Haute Savoie where she could take in other children as paying guests. We arrived in Haute Savoie one evening in September 1950, after a long train journey across France, and moved into a rented chalet, *La Pitchounette*, overlooking the mountain village of St. Gervais-les-Bains. The following morning I was enthralled to open my bed-room shutters and see the long green grass, each blade with a silver tip of frost, growing right up to the house walls. The whole valley was silver grey and dark green in the morning sunshine. I knew I was going to like it there.

And so it turned out. The next four years were paradise. We three children were joined by three others: a boy and two girls of our own age. Each winter morning we would set off to school, *L'Assumption*, three kilometres away in the village—with our toboggans

Camping in the garden of our house in St. Gervais les Bains, aged five.

In the Alpine meadows of Haute Savoie, aged seven.

slithering and sliding down the icy road and our schoolbooks on our backs. We hardly ever saw a car in those days. Each evening we would trudge back up the road home with our toboggans in tow, hissing and crunching behind us. I used to love this walk, laughing and singing and playing our favourite game of standing in a line and all falling together face down into the deep snow. Above all I used to look forward to arriving home and drinking frothy hot milk which had just been milked and boiled. I could not help but admire my mother at this time, whom I saw as a person of rare beauty and courage. Apart from the love and care of a mother she also provided the material support to supplement the modest income provided by my father.

At Christmas all six children would dress up, the girls with bows in their hair, and toboggan down to the village church for midnight mass. I think we must have been quite a sight by the time we arrived, but no one really cares about such things in the mountains. After the long toboggan ride in the freezing air it was difficult not to fall asleep in the warm welcoming interior of the church, and we would nudge each other throughout the service to stay awake. The interior of the church was slightly Byzantine and decorated with a rustic splendour that befitted the mountains. Walking back home after mass was hard work but it was such a pleasure to sing carols in the gently falling snow or under the bright Alpine starlight. The real treat on Christmas Eve was to eat the *Petit Jesus* cakes dipped in hot chocolate before collapsing into bed.

In the summer we would pick *pisenlit* for our salad from the roadside and rhubarb from the garden for puddings. We also used to pick daffodils beside the *telepherique* at Le Bettex which we sold to tourists. How proud I was of the few centimes I earned this way. There was no television in those days in the Alps and we would amuse ourselves playing charades at home and conducting endless singing meetings. We would spend the long summer evenings visiting the surrounding farms and playing marbles with our ruddy-cheeked little friends who lived above the cows in their Savoyard farm chalets.

All this ended in 1955 when I was nine, for my uncle, whose wife had died and who had always had a soft spot for his young cousin, my mother, proposed to her and became my stepfather. So we moved back to the North and joined his four children—Mariette, Michel, Patrice, and Stefane—who were now twice related to me, first as cousins and second as stepbrothers and -sister.

My uncle was known as the "Cashmere King" of Northern France because he owned one of the largest and most successful businesses in France for cashmere yarn. He was so engrossed in fibre yarns that each Sunday in church he would concentrate not on higher things, but on the fibre composition of the coats in front of him. We used to giggle when we saw him rock backwards and forwards so that he could "accidentally" brush against someone's jacket. One Sunday his curiosity so overcame him that, with his head leaning back so that he could see down through his pince-nez, he started to rub the jacket of the lady sitting in front of him. She never sat near him again.

My uncle's involvement in this luxurious fashion textile could have been the beginning of my interest in the world of fashion design, but, although I enjoyed the silky softness of the yarn, it was its awful smell that I remember the most. In his office there were shelves packed with samples of the hair of the Mongolian goat from which cashmere wool is derived. The samples showed the hair at its different stages of treatment, the first of which was nothing more than an oily mass.

My uncle's huge house was in Roubaix Tourcoing. It needed to be huge for we formed a family of seven children between seven and fourteen years of age. My uncle was a stickler for elocution. At mealtimes he would sit at the end of our long table and interrupt the conversation, not to comment on the topic, but to insist on correct pronunciation. "Non," he would cry, "Si'il vous plait…Eu pas Eie!" In fact he was a stickler for all things precise and used to indulge himself with a huge array of clocks all over the house that he would adjust minutely every day. Like many of his contemporaries, he was a reserved man and rarely showed his affection in a physical way. After the relaxed country life in the Alps, our move back to town life was not easy and despite all the care and material luxury of a French middle-class family, we three at first felt a little like outsiders in my uncle's home.

At school I was beginning the more serious phase of my education. This was at a Dominican convent in Lille called *St. Jeanne d'Arc*. It was next to the local *lycée*, the state school. I envied the lycée children, who seemed wild and uninhibited but the north of France was very restrictive and no child from a *bonne famille* went to a lycée. The nuns at the convent were altogether different from the *Corbeaux*. For one thing they wore white and had open faces. There was a wonderful mother superior called Marie-Jeanne. The school buildings were built in beautiful cream-coloured stone with dark grey shiny roof tiles—the same colouring as the *châteaux* of the Loire. The grounds were picturesque and the whole place felt like a family home.

A school trip at age thirteen to the Brussels Atomium with my physics teacher, one of the nuns from St. Jeanne d'Arc.

With the guidance of these kind women and without much to distract me I threw myself into my studies. I loved mathematics and Latin. I did well academically but within a year or so paid the social penalty of maintaining a position in a class where I was two years younger than everyone else. Two years is a huge gulf at twelve, and all the other girls seemed so much more mature. One in particular, Sophie, seemed so perfectly at ease with her Côte d'Azur suntan, her perfect hair, and perfect compact little figure—I was almost six feet tall and rather gauche. Recently I bumped into Sophie again. It was in the lift in Harrods. She didn't recognise me but there she was with her perfect hair and her two perfect *bon chic bon genre* children. I smiled to myself at how I used to worry all those years ago.

However, the worry was real enough at the time. In the late fifties Northern France was very bourgeois and as a child of divorced parents I was generally *persona non grata*. The net effect of having divorced parents and being two years younger than my class-mates, fragile, very tall, thin, and flat chested was that I was very socially ill at ease. Life here in Lille was very different from the mountains where everything was clear and taken at face value. I did not speak the same social language as others and, being unable to play little social "games," it was difficult to communicate my feelings. I became shy and awkward. From this period in my life I think I developed a way to overcome these feel-ings of discomfort—I was confident in my schoolwork and buried myself in the com-fort and security of study. I carried this into my working life as a designer where, as an adult, I would divert adversity into my work. Through the years people have called me a workaholic, but whatever a workaholic is, I am actually driven by something really rather simple.

During the school holidays my time was meticulously divided between my mother and my father. My family situation now became a little comical and takes some explaining. My father had married his cousin's ex-wife, Tatie, whose maiden name was Chevalier. His cousin, who had been his business partner (and was also my godfa-ther) had the same surname, Baheux, as my father. So Tatie did not need to change her surname on remarriage and nor did her chil-dren from her first marriage. So Michel-Jean, Armand, Cecile, and Remy, my new step-brothers and -sister, all had the same sur-name as me and my sister and brother but from different fathers. Years later my sister Nicole married Tatie's nephew and became a Chevalier-Baheux-Chevalier, the first and last parts of the name being from different branches of the same family.

In Port-au-Bessin, as in Lille, I joined four cousins-cum-stepbrothers and -sisters to make seven children in the house but I could also at times feel the odd one out. In both my mother's and father's homes I was deeply loved and affectionately known as *La Petite Catherine*. I am told I was inquisi-tive, lively, a little wicked, and became terribly excited about small things. I was extremely affectionate and was born with an unconditional love and trust of life. But I was physically fragile and because I had an intuitive insight into others' feelings could easily become overwhelmed with emotion. I would then withdraw into myself and cry out my *dérangement*. When this happened no one knew what to do with me or how to approach me. It still happens today.

The countryside around my father's house in Normandy was spectacular. In the late summer the orchards turned a golden colour, and on a still day the Atlantic air turned to a warm mist. Above all I remem-ber the vast and peaceful flatness of the Nor-mandy sands, which evoked for me an immense feeling of freedom. Visits to my father were also a gastronomic experience. Tatie introduced me to French cooking at its best and I found her cooking irresistible but unfortunately the rich creamy Calvados sauces did not agree with my digestion, which was already upset by the strained rela-tionship between my father and mother, and I spent most of the time in the bathroom.

I did, however, get on very well with my father's St. Emilion. Like all Frenchmen who love wine, he bought it directly in barrels from the vineyard. We would enjoy siphoning the wine from these barrels because of course you had to take a mouthful to fill the siphon.

My father's side of the family were serious *bon-viveurs* of the shooting, hunting, and fishing kind. This style of living went back to the 1700s and was mixed with an equally strong representation of monseigneurs.

Shortly after my seventeenth birthday I was at the University of Lille studying philosophy, and my adult life began. It seems as though I skipped the rebellious years of adolescence: I had become so protective of my mother that I did not want to tease her in this way. One day at the wedding of my cousin Chantal, I met Jean-Pierre. He was tall with dark hair and deep aquamarine eyes, and like many Corsicans was slightly wild and ruggedly romantic. He was twenty-six, and I was flattered by his attention. We fell in love, and at eighteen I became engaged. There followed four engagement parties, one in Lille for my stepfather's friends, one in Normandy with my father, one in the Alps at the holiday home of my mother, and one in Marseille with Jean-Pierre's family. The latter were a handsome clan, erudite and rather wealthy.

In order to be nearer to Jean-Pierre I decided to finish my degree at the University in Aix-en-Provence. My family extended even to this corner of France where I stayed with the Sevin family who are related to me on my mother's side. This lovable but totally eccentric family seemed to personify the Provençal character (Pagnol readers will be familiar with this) which compared starkly with the somewhat colder and severe North, and I enjoyed their company immensely. My great-uncle Achile was a wonderful character with a long white beard. He would each day declare his love for me and write me poems, one of which never ceases to touch me.

Petite princesse lointaine,
tu rêves de bouquets de fleurs,
de sonorités, de couleurs,
de mer bleue et de vastes plaines . . .

Tandis qu'aux heures incertaines
dans le soir gris tombent nos pleurs,
tu ne rêves que de bonheurs;
Comment les saisir à mains pleines,

Comment les conserver? Surtout,
comment garder, suprême atout
l'enthousiasme et la jeunesse?

Ah! pour que nulle heure, des jours
à venir, jamais ne te blesse;
En toi, garde un immense amour!

ACHILE SEVIN, AIX EN PROVENCE
JUIN 1960

This is my translation into English:

Little Princess far away,
You dream of flower bouquets,
of sounds, of colours,
of blue seas, of vast plains . . .

While during the uncertain grey hours
of evening our tears fall,
you dream only of happiness
and how to seize it with open hands,

How do you cherish it? Most of all,
how do you keep it, this supreme asset of
enthusiasm and youth?

Ah! So that no hour of any day
ever comes to hurt you,
keep your heart full of love!

Here in the clear air of Provence I could forget the cruel burden of my parents' divorce. My memories of Aix were of long walks in the thyme- and rosemary-scented hills of Mont St. Victoire, late parties followed by early morning coffee and *callisons* (almond biscuits), long discussions with my tutors about philosophy, and eventually, in the cold light of day, breaking off my engagement.

Jean-Pierre was delightful but I knew in my heart we would not make each other happy. As the months passed and the wedding grew nearer I knew I was going to have to summon my courage. With a few weeks to go I called it off. The Corsicans were furious as was my mother who had had some difficulty assembling vast numbers of family from all corners of France. I was sent back to Lille in disgrace. I finished my degree and decided I would work my way to the United States via England.

One of the reasons I had decided to visit England arose after a wonderful dinner I had at Aix. A fellow student at the University, an English boy called Andrew, invited me with a group of his friends to a dinner hosted by his father at one of Aix's best restaurants. I spoke little English at the time and when the dinner was over I found, to my embarrassment, that I did not know how to thank Andrew's father. Quite suddenly I felt that my education had been so abstract that in real life I fell at the first practical hurdle.

The first stop on my journey to the United States was at the end of the District Line in London at a place called Upminster Bridge. Through the University at Aix I had found a job teaching French at a school in Hornchurch. I had travelled from France in a coach and had the misfortune to sit next to a very sickly looking Englishman, who I think tried to make advances towards me but whose English I could not understand. In later years I found that many things said to me in England went over my head, which in the hothouse atmosphere of couture was probably a good thing.

I arrived at Victoria Station with an enormous suitcase and was met by a representative of the school who put me on the tube. I had never been in an underground train before, and it was quite a novelty. On leaving the tube I followed a map to the house where I was to stay. This was owned by a kind elderly lady, Edna, who used to cook me "tea" which I discovered was her one and only evening meal. It consisted, apart from cups and cups of tea, of slices of tinned corned beef with some lettuce and tomato to which was added some creamy dressing from a bottle.

The class I taught contained twenty sixteen-year-old boys. I myself was twenty-one, and the lesson consisted of me speaking French and each boy replying in French. Unfortunately, there were no classrooms to conduct these lessons, and I had to make do with teaching on a rather dimly lit staircase. Looking back I wonder how the whole thing remained so well-mannered, but I taught this class three times a week for a year and was much congratulated by the headmaster who gave me a glowing reference.

Soon after my arrival in London I also met a titled young man, Randolph, whose country house I once visited to meet his parents. Here breakfast was a lavish affair with large silver dishes containing scrambled eggs, bacon, tomatoes, kidneys, and all sorts of other things all set out on a mahogany sideboard in a large dining room. The contrast between breakfast at Randolph's house and the lovely Edna's tea gave me a wonderful perspective of the English class system of which I had heard but never before witnessed. In France food is not such a defining factor between classes.

The mid-sixties were the height of "Swinging London." For many fashion designers this was (and still is) a time of immense inspiration. However, I was not at all focused on clothes at the time. Although I recall a photograph of myself in 1965 wearing a floral trouser suit and bowler hat and smoking a pipe, which, against the regulated *bourgeoisie* of Northern France, felt like great fun, it was the freedom of the era that appealed to me not its clothes. One could be oneself without being judged.

In April I moved from Hornchurch to a tiny flat over a butcher's shop on Stratford Road in Earl's Court. I shared this minuscule flat with two "Georgie Girls," as they were called in the sixties. We had one bedroom between us which I found became a bit too noisy when they invited their boyfriends to stay the night. They never seemed to stop singing "I Can't Get No Satisfaction." By that winter I could no longer cope with the antiquated heating system in this little flat, which left me freezing all night and still thawing out until about noon the next day, and so I moved to Devonshire Place where I shared a more spacious flat with two girls, one of whom was a physiotherapist, Anna, and the other an opera singer, Sally. I could not really afford this flat and I used to survive on boiled eggs and my daily lunch at the canteen of the school in Hornchurch. Early in 1967 Sally introduced me to a young law student named John. I remember it was February for you always remember the month when you fall in love.

Mid-1960s style.

It was about this time that I also met a philosophy lecturer at London University, Jean-Marie, who persuaded me to take my studies further, and later that year I returned to Lille for a postgraduate *maitrise* in Aesthetics and in particular the study of Edwin Panowski. John and I were deeply in love but we reluctantly agreed that I had to finish my *maitrise* and he his law finals, and so I left for France. I suppose in the back of my mind this was also a way of testing John's feelings. I knew he was right for me, but men take such a long time to acknowledge their feelings.

I arrived back in the North and found myself in the midst of a political turmoil. This was a time of serious social unrest in France. At the university, effigies of de Gaulle were daubed with slogans ridiculing his new legislation on strikes. These new laws had caused many grievances among groups such as the miners in Pas-de-Calais who had earlier supported him. Throughout the country, and especially in the mining and industrial Pas-de-Calais, the working class wages had for some years been falling behind those of other social groups.

Throughout the spring of 1968, *Le Monde* carried stories of strikes which it said had started to break out all over France. At the university the leader of the Student Union, a tall charismatic mustachioed young man called Olivier, gave a two-hour speech explaining that de Gaulle's regime was ignoring Parliament (a cardinal sin in French politics) in matters such as the building of gold reserves and nuclear weapons. Even the most placid students were stirred by these speeches. The general mood both at Lille and in other universities was for revolution, which is a very emotive word in France. By May 1968 the whole situation erupted. Helped partly by police over-reaction and partly by activists, probably with sinister motives of their own, strikes and street riots spread from France throughout many parts of Europe and even into this normally tranquil part of northern France (much to the disgust of my stepfather, who was a staunch Gaullist). However de Gaulle managed to calm things down, although it was many years before France recovered, and indeed the President himself was obliged to resign the following year.

I succeeded with top honours in my *maitrise* and left France and the seething politics to return to London that August. John too had passed his exams and had started work as a solicitor with a large city firm. I knew the moment I arrived back at Victoria Station I had made the right decision and in June 1969 we were married. The venue for our marriage was chosen after some deliberation. We located a point midway between my father in Normandy, my mother in Lille,

and John's parents in London. This point was in fact somewhere in the English Channel, so we chose the nearest town, Le Touquet. All my family came, including both my parents who, after much persuasion, agreed to put aside their grievances for the day. It was actually the first time I had seen my parents together since I was four. The English contingent, waiting quietly in the church in their uniform of top hats and morning suits, made a comic contrast to the French who burst into the church in a jovial manner intent on enjoying themselves to the full. I was not looking forward to this day as I knew I could be rekindling old family feuds but in the event everyone was charming.

When we returned to London we bought a tiny house on Masbro Road, near Brook Green in West London. It was a pretty street occupied partly by older inhabitants, many of whom had lived in the neighbourhood since before the war, and young new arrivals like ourselves. I remember seeing a young bearded man a few doors away who John said had just started a company called Virgin Records. I took a job at the French Embassy Lecture Department, and then later I took over the Film Department at the French Institute. The Institute was next to the *lycée* in South Kensington where I later taught eighteenth-century French literature to eighteen-year-old boys. Since I knew nothing about French literature I would spend each evening learning what I was going to teach the next day. My bluffing was so successful that I was engaged to teach private lessons in French literature to the French Ambassador's son.

In May 1971 our first daughter, Naomi, was born and eighteen months later, in November 1972, Marianne arrived. The babies were pure bliss and John a devoted father. I was overwhelmed by the pureness and fragility of the children and the intense emotion of love they stirred within me. It was a love untinged by any emotional stress—a new experience in my life. I embarked on an English middle-class life of country weekends, dinner parties, and children's parties.

However, I was, not for the first time in my life, the odd one out. It was obvious that the innate traditions and nuances of the English middle class were foreign to me. Despite great kindness shown by John's friends, his love, and the joy of our babies, at times I felt isolated in his family. To compensate for this I started to decorate the house—sawing wood, cutting tiles, and decorating.

How do I describe John? He was every foreigner's idea of a perfect English gentleman. He was a generous, fair-minded idealist, who, in the days of the empire, would have been an inspirational force. He had broadminded views on a united European community, which was unusual in the early seventies, and he was an active member of numerous overseas development programmes in his spare time. He had been made a partner at his law firm and had a bright future ahead. Perhaps the best insight into John would be a

At Masbro Road with my new baby daughter, Naomi, June 1971.

snapshot of that fateful day when we left London in the summer of 1975.

That morning he was energetically filling up our Volkswagen Beetle and humming loudly to himself, his wavy hair all tousled as usual. In went the suitcases and several plastic bags overflowing with clothing, his tennis racket, squash racket, clarinet, sheet music, copies of the *New Statesman* not yet read, correspondence to catch up on to Jerome (a Nigerian friend from VSO days), a briefcase of office work, baby food, two babies, and me. Off we charged to Newhaven. Three days later John was dead.

Widowhood

After the ambulance had taken John away the night became unbearably still. I could feel the echo of what had happened reverberating in the stillness. I didn't know what lay ahead for me—what pain, grief, or struggles. At four o'clock in the morning in the darkness before dawn I felt a power of life surge deep inside me like a knee-jerk reaction to John's death. My senses sharpened to a frightening intensity. When someone gave me a cup of coffee the intensity of taste exploded in my mouth. It reminded me of the tea I was given the night Naomi was born at Queen Charlotte's Hospital—also at about four in the morning—I will never forget the intensity of its taste. The joy of birth and the tragedy of death seem to focus the senses profoundly.

Grief for me was a private thing and not one I felt like sharing. Different people at the time expressed their grief in their own way. Some who had had pain before wanted me to come into their world, but I wanted to be left alone. I could not be alone of course because almost immediately people started to collect in the village. In the hours after John's death I had to face telling his and my family what had happened. My mother arranged for the children to go to the North while the ritual of death took place.

I remember in a haze going through the ghastly details of registering the death at the *Mairie*, the visit to the morgue where the warm vital human being I loved had been "put away" in a refrigerator. I remember the faces of John's parents puffed with tears. I remember the triviality of being worried about my stepmother coming and meeting with my own mother. My senses within this haze became strangely acute: I remember the beautiful colour of the haystacks in the fields. I remember sitting and eating with people at the same table where the night before John and I had enjoyed our dinner party. I remember the endless talk of people explaining their incredulity at his death. I remember my stepsister saying to me how lucky I had been to have loved somebody—it made me cross. I remember an aunt, herself a widow of fifteen years, telling me how one never gets over it—it made my anger increase. Another aunt told me I would survive because I was sensitive to the little things in life. I didn't know what she meant at the time but I do now. People were looking at me and thinking "What is she going through?" I had, literally overnight, become a freak.

I drove back to London in the Beetle. In our little house time stood still. As the days passed I started to pack John's things into cardboard boxes. I mended one of his shirts. I cannot describe how it felt except to say it was the same sensation as being violently homesick. It came in waves oddly similar to the waves of pain in childbirth, overpowering and beyond control. I clung to something I had read in *Gift of the Sea* by Anne Morrow Lindbergh (New York: Random House, 1992.):

> *We have so little faith in the ebb and flow of love of relationships—we leap at the flow of the tide and resist in terror its ebb—we are afraid it will never return. We insist on permanency, on duration, on continuity, when the only continuity possible in life as in love is in growth, in fluidity.*
>
> *Security in a relationship lies neither in looking back to what it was in nostalgia, or*

*anticipation, but living in the present relation-
ship and accepting it as it is now. For relationships, too, must be like islands—one must
accept them for what they are here and now,
within their limits—islands surrounded and
interrupted by the sea, continually visited and
abandoned by the tides. One must accept the
security of the winged life, of ebb and flow, of
intermittency.*

*Each cycle of the wave is valid; each cycle
of the tide is valid; each cycle of a relationship
is valid.*

I was living in a numb oblivion trying to
be as cheerful as possible with the children.
Marianne's birthday passed, and then Christmas came, each a kind of torture for all three
of us. It was an extraordinary feeling, for the
person around whom our lives revolved was
gone—we revolved around nothing.

After a time I started to write a diary. I
found a spiral-bound notebook that John had
used to make notes while he read a book by
Aleksandr Solzhenitsyn on holiday. I opened
the first page written in his neat methodical
handwriting. It was the last thing he had written. My throat went tight as I read his words:

*I developed a theory . . . that there is no such
thing as human happiness—either it's unat-
tainable or it's illusory. Well, after I'd finished,
I was handed a note from a student . . . "I'm
in love and I am happy." What do you say to
that? What could I say?*

When the numbness had passed it was
replaced by an ache, not like a headache but a
whole bodyache. I mechanically went through
the motions of waking up, dressing the children, taking them to nursery school, doing the
shopping, cooking, feeding and bathing the
children, and going to bed where I would lie
awake sometimes for three nights in a row.
After Christmas I sent the children to my
mother in the Alps and decided I would stay
in Aix for a few days while I tried to stop taking the sleeping pills I had been prescribed. I
did stop and for a fleeting moment in the clear
air of Provence I started to feel angry.

In Aix I stayed with the Sevin family and
found great friendship with my cousins. During that week I talked a lot with my second
cousin Didier and I felt a huge up-welling of
emotion. After the weeks of being strong for
the children I broke down. I think I came to
Aix on purpose to do this. It was where I had
felt free as a student, free for the first time
from the stigma of my parents' divorce, and it
was where I knew I could explode. Going to
Aix was cathartic, and when Didier saw how
much I loved Provence he asked me if I
would come and live in Aix near the family
where they could look after me. I thought
about it as I returned to London. By the time
I arrived back to the house I had decided to
take up his offer.

When I first came to London, it was
intended to be the first step in my journey to
the United States. Now, once again, I stayed
longer than I had anticipated, for my neigh-
bours, Mary and Richard, who had known
me and John for all the years we had been
married introduced me to the man who
would become my next husband.

In the months following John's death I
changed. This sounds like an obvious statement but it was the *kind* of change that mattered. First, time passed in slow motion. Each
three-month period felt as long as a year. Like
after the birth of a child one's own time is
temporarily dismantled and replaced by the

newborn rhythm of sleeping, waking, and feeding. Second, my view of the world changed. I saw people differently, not with criticism, but as if through tinted glasses. Third, things that had preoccupied me before seemed very small and insignificant. French middle-class values which I never held strongly seemed trivial. My half-adopted middle-class English values were no longer part of my life. My whole perspective was altering. I started to understand things for the first time purely on the merit of my convictions. I became aware that there were huge gaps in my understanding. I did not know what should fill them, just that they were there—a kind of naiveté. Fourth, my senses were acute. They were painfully sharp.

I was also aware that I was a curiosity. Some people would invite me to dinner to look at me as one would look at an animal in a zoo. Others used the rather pathetic imagery of the "swinging sixties" and told me my experience had made me "real." Others, rather unexpectedly (since they were good friends of John's) started making advances towards me. Some more sincere friends thought it was time for me to set my grief aside. My neighbour Mary was one of these, and one day her husband Richard, who was a furniture designer, invited me to an exhibition of his work in Covent Garden. Mary wanted me to go to meet a couple of her bachelor friends.

I did not enjoy socialising anymore and on that January day it was raining so I almost didn't go. But I reluctantly made the effort for Richard. I only met one of Mary's friends. His name was Saïd. I never found out who the second person was for there was only ever going to be one.

Mary had given me a sort of "dating agency profile" of who Saïd was. It went something like this: Persian, thirty-one, gorgeous and very popular with the girls, unmarried, public-school educated and all that, a visiting lecturer at a London art school, ran his own successful business, led a very modest lifestyle.

But when I met him what really touched me was how different he was. He understood so much. I had felt such pain, I was so ready to be spoilt and he was so prepared to be there, to listen. He did not pretend to understand everything; he let me mourn John at my own pace. Above all he was not frightened of me—as a tall Gallic young widow with two children I found I had become a frightening figure that separated the men from the boys.

As the weeks passed I tried to keep pace with Saïd. In metaphorical terms, he could run and I could hardly walk and it hurt to try. But I was in love, he wanted me to run, and I desperately wanted to catch up with him. Life had started again. During those early days I could only marvel at the beautiful flowers, the dizzy weekends above the Spanish Steps in Rome, skiing on the Hahnenkamm, the silly games with the children. All three of us fell in love with him and he with us. I telephoned Didier and told him I was staying in London.

The Chelsea Design Company *1976–81*

ONE STITCH AT A TIME

In 1973 my mother-in-law had made a bet with her three children (and me) that she would give £15 to any one of us who gave up smoking. This was easy for me because I never really smoked anyway so I won the bet. I don't know why, but I bought this little Elna sewing machine. I had never sewn much before and had always been seen as the intellectual of the family rather than someone with manual skills. It was *farfelu*—bravado. I soon found that I loved sewing and I would sew anything for anyone just for the pleasure of it. I was intrigued by the technical process of stitching and making as well as pleased to have a continuous supply of new clothes for the girls. It was not the joy of a dressmaker nor the creative thrill of a designer. It was purely technical devotion.

After John's death, during the spring of 1976, when the children were at school and Saïd had gone to lecture or to his office, I was alone in the house and I found every corner full of memories of the wonderful years with John. I could not contain these and start a new life at the same time. I decided I had to move away from Masbro Road and do something with my time. When I discussed this with Saïd, his first reaction was to start a business, one that would leave me enough time to look after the children. He was painfully aware of my lack of commercial experience and so we discussed how such a thing would start. We talked and we, or rather he, made a plan. I'll never forget his words that night:

"You're going to make the Rolls Royce of children's clothes." It frightened me because he was so convinced.

I have to say in my mind I did not have any such plan at all. Sewing to me was just a kind of therapy. At first I threw myself into my new work with a vigour that was fuelled by a need to control my pain and sorrow. I loved the reassuring throb of the machine and the tactile sensation of the cloth under my fingers. I loved to experiment with new ideas, however small. I turned a spare room in the basement into a little workshop. Saïd made me a table with a board over two filing cabinets on which I put my Elna sewing machine and reference (pattern-cutting) books. About two months later this had borne fruit and I had a tiny "collection" of clothes. These were intricate angel-tops and pinafores with edge binding. This was as much as I knew how to make at the time but they were lovingly made in the best fabrics.

So I started my "commercial life" in the summer of 1976, walking up and down the Kings Road in Chelsea, trying to sell my little children's dresses from a basket like a gypsy. I had no idea people could be so rude. I still blush at my naiveté. I would literally knock on doors, one of which was a shop called Small Wonder in the Kings Road. When I was actually allowed into this shop I was so nervous that I dropped all the clothes and had to scramble on the floor to retrieve my precious samples. The owner, a blond lady who seemed very polished, suggested that I make her a sample of a size-four corduroy girl's skirt. It was September 1976 when I received my first order. It was for seven navy and seven brown skirts in seven different sizes. This was my first experience in grading patterns from one size to the next. I sold them for 70p each. However, Saïd pointed out that it was the experience and not the profit (or loss in this case) that mattered.

I would carry my basket from Portobello Road to South Molton Street and, despite raising my prices to a more realistic level, little by little the "business" began to work. Something was appealing to these buyers. It may have been to do with the combination of traditional English design with a French cut: my little dresses were much longer and narrower than any other little girls' dresses on the market at the time. When I visited these shops I was of course able to see the competition while I nervously waited to see the buyer. These were perfectly made and executed clothes but they did not discourage me because they looked as though they came from a factory. One of the first things I noticed about my "taste" was that I loved to play with light—a quality that the factory-made clothes seemed to have lost. I sold each basketful and anxiously returned home to start making more.

I decided to sell some furniture that had belonged to my grandmother and that I had kept in storage. It was antique Provençale furniture: a three-seat sofa, two dressers and a cupboard all beautifully inlaid in oak. I did it against Saïd's advice, and it broke my heart, but I used the money to buy my first semi-industrial sewing machine, a Bernina. The need to make the clothes had become an addiction, I really only wanted to sell the dresses so that I could use the proceeds to learn more.

The little girls' dresses I was making to order became less and less my own design. In fact I was beginning to rather dislike them. It occurred to me that if only I could speak to the customers themselves, I was sure they would want what I designed and not the awful things the buyers asked me to do. The buyers seemed to want to replace the lightness and simplicity of the design with something they called "hanger appeal." I decided wholesaling was not for me and we decided to look for a studio as well as a new house away from Masbro Road.

In those days all real designers had "studios" where clients visited by appointment. We did find some rooms in Caroline Terrace in Belgravia, but it was then that we stumbled upon a completely dilapidated house on

65 Sydney Street, Chelsea, London SW3.

The house we bought in February 1977, because it was near the lycée *where the girls were at school. It used to be an off-licence and was derelict but ideal for a studio to start The Chelsea Design Company. Some years later I wrote off for one of those "check the history of your house" services. It appears that in 1881, 65 Sydney Street, Chelsea, was owned by one Eleanor George. She was a widow, she had two daughters, and she was a seamstress to the court of Queen Victoria.*

Sydney Street in Chelsea, with a disused off-licence on the ground floor. By this time both my girls were attending the *lycée* in South Kensington so this ruin of a house, which looked like a wreck to everyone else, looked like heaven to me. We bought the house in early 1977 and did all the shopfitting ourselves with a budget of £200. It consisted of a huge table, which we bought from a curtain dry cleaners, my new sewing machine at one end, and a partition separating the shop area where I put my samples and stock on racks. The partition had a pattern of little holes in it, about the size of golf balls, so that I could work at the back and see the front at the same time. I remember the first customers who came in were rather amused by the set-up which was half shop and half studio workroom. In the first week my turnover was £22 for two angel-tops and a little pinafore. I think in the second week it slumped to £14. My first sale was such a surprise that I had to leave the customer alone in the shop and run to my flat to find a plastic bag to put it in.

During this first year I spent each day totally alone, aside from the rather infrequent visits of customers and people asking the way to the Kings Road. I wish I could say that I was working to a planned strategy but in fact I was simply following each day as it came. I was doing everything myself—pattern cutting, making up, pressing, pricing, displaying, selling—I hesitate to use the word designing. I had had a very rigid academic education and I approached these new projects the only way I knew how, which many people would say was too thorough. Even at this early date my determination must have shown because I would often hear people tell me "Don't work *too* hard." There were still

nights when I could not sleep and I would while away my time studying, cutting, and sewing. I recall how upset I was when my grading was out by one sixteenth of an inch. My grief was consumed in such tiny details.

I was totally unaware of whether the work I was doing was leading to anything successful. I had no idea what was going on in the fashion world. The whole notion of movements in the fashion world, such as the New Romantic of the early 1980s, simply passed me by. I didn't go shopping, I didn't even read magazines. My life for the next five years was totally immersed in these children's clothes. I was distantly aware that I was out of synchronisation with reality but I had found something that made me feel I could control the pain of John's death without clinging to Saïd or the children. I was centred in myself and only aware of my survival, but I now know that this period was of immense value to me. I was developing an eye for fitting through my tiny clients and I was learning body proportioning through doing endless minute adjustments.

I have always loved babies and young children, and there were moments of joy and fun. We had a small TV monitor in the shop where we showed videotapes of cartoons so that children would keep still while being measured for their sailor suits. The shop was more and more busy and quite chaotic, especially on Saturdays. Several famous people brought their children, and the atmosphere was often a pure delight. My own girls loved to model the clothes.

The other pleasure was the lovely people who had started working for me. Helen was pregnant when she answered our advertisement for a machinist in 1978, and shortly

after that time she separated from her husband. She took a full-time job about a year later but continued to work for us on a piece-work basis. Helen went on to put her son through private education for the next twenty years entirely on the hard work she did for us in the evenings and on weekends. Carmelita also answered an advertisement for a machinist at that time. Carmelita is Portuguese (from Madeira) and after many years in England still hardly speaks English, but her character, like her work, is full of generosity. Over the years she has turned her hand to all sorts of projects and grown with us from our humble beginnings. I know that she has been approached by several other companies and ex-staff to move away from us but like all the best people she is not just generous but loyal. Susannah joined us about three months after we started. I don't think Susannah needed to work because her husband was a successful estate agent at the time; she is just very good with her hands and obviously enjoyed the craft side of what we do. Today Susannah still makes the most

top

Naomi and Marianne, 1979.

We could never make enough of these sailor suits and dresses, either in navy-and-white cotton ticking, as shown here, or in navy velvet. They were immensely popular here in London as they had been in the days of my parents' childhood in France.

left

Naomi and Marianne with friends Gemma and Alice, 1979.

Drop-waisted sailor dresses in navy cotton drill.

beautiful handmade rosettes, and although she pops in and out so that we hardly ever see her, I know there have been dozens and dozens of brides whose dresses were made more beautiful by Susannah's expert handicraft. The fourth person who started when I started was Hennie, whom I first met when I was married to John. Hennie is one of those people who is competent at everything, and Saïd actually offered her a partnership at the beginning which she (probably most wisely) turned down. It was Hennie who joined in to help me deliver my first order of babies' clothes and she is still helping me today although she has her own successful business. I became very attached to all these people and I used to love sharing minute details with them. I was gradually emerging from my shell, "one stitch at a time"—at least in my professional life.

As time passed the work became less trial and error and more deliberate intent. My first venture into adult designs was designing maternity dresses. Anyone who has designed children's clothes will know that maternity dresses could be seen as a purely technical progression from children's clothes. Children have very big tummies for their height and if you grade them up to an adult size you actually have something resembling a pregnant woman. I used to wear the smocks to get the feel of them and would inevitably be asked when the baby was due. Maybe this eventually convinced me that it was time to move on.

By 1981 we had diminished the children's clothes to a capsule collection, and started a proper collection of day, cocktail, and evening dresses. During that next season things just exploded. Our one telephone never stopped ringing, people would come in and stay on the doormat because the shop was too full, the magazines noticed us, and it only increased the frenzy when *Vogue* featured a modest jabot-fronted polka dot day dress in the spring. We were astonished at how successful the business had become. In fact everywhere we looked we saw the word *success*. That August we closed for three weeks while we re-shopfitted to cater for the extra clients. It made little difference for when we reopened in the autumn, we still had people changing in the middle of the shop, the back hall, and even the back garden.

I was no longer making clothes as a therapy; I had fallen in love with the process of designing and making them. However I was still reluctant to call myself a designer. In Paris people would laugh at anyone putting their name on a shopfront and calling themselves a designer without the skill and background to prove it. In deference to this inexperience we called our business "The Chelsea Design Company," rather than "Catherine Walker," the name being simply a description of where we were and what we did.

Before long, my diary was filled with names of famous people I had only ever read about. However it was not the fact they were famous that thrilled me but the fact that their demands allowed me to expand the technical frontiers of my little world. It was exhilarating and the more I did, the more I learned, although my philosophy was still "one stitch at a time." The clothes were improving in leaps and bounds and I was now buying fabric from the top suppliers in Lyons, lace from Calais, and silk from Como.

Although we had stopped the maternity range we did not discontinue it quite as quickly as we had planned, for in November that year we received an order from someone who was expecting her first baby. It was, of course, the new Princess of Wales.

above

AUTUMN/WINTER COLLECTION 1981

Green silk crepe de chine smock dress.

HRH The Princess of Wales leaving St. Mary's Hospital after the birth of HRH Prince William of Wales, 21 June 1982.

Photographer: Tim Graham

left

Oyster silk satin faconné shirtwaister.

Commissioned by HRH The Princess of Wales. Official portrait by Snowdon of HRH The Princess of Wales with Prince William on TRH's first wedding anniversary, 29 July 1982.

Although the Princess usually approached me through her lady-in-waiting, on this occasion we received a request via Vogue for a "beige or cream or pale blue dress for a formal portrait of someone special." It was as vague as that and we could only assume it was for the Princess. Since we had her measurements we were able to make this oyster silk faconné dress which we saw on every front page a day later.

Photographer: Lord Snowdon/Camera Press

Drop-waisted dress with draped bodice in ice blue Abraham silk satin.

Commissioned by HRH The Princess of Wales for the film premiere of *Indiana Jones*, London, February 1984.

This dress was worn in February 1984 for the film premiere of Indiana Jones *in aid of the Prince's Trust in London, and again that year at the Royal Tournament.*

I suppose I should remember this dress for the press it received: "With just one dress . . . Diana has changed the silhouette of maternity clothes," reported the Evening Standard. *Fashion editor Liz Smith commented "I remember marvelling at one . . . satin dress the Princess appeared in when pregnant, predicting perfectly correctly that its side-swathed line would change the shape of maternity dresses by dropping the emphasis from above to below the bulge."*
I later learned that the trend had been copied by maternity shops throughout the country.

What I actually remember this dress for, however, was a different kind of "press" that it received. At that time our staff was so small that I still steam-pressed many of the designs before they left the premises. I remember steaming this dress with good reason, because when it was finished and ready to go, I gave it a final press and to my horror, a heat-induced mark appeared on the front of the loosely pleated skirt. We ordered a new length from Zurich and replaced the panel within forty-eight hours, just in time for the film premiere.

Photograph by Photographers International

Ivory silk satin mandarin collar dress.

Commissioned by HRH The Princess of Wales. Official portrait by Snowdon of HRH The Princess of Wales with HRH Prince Harry, October 1984.

There is a tradition dating back to the days of Queen Mary or even Queen Alexandra of wearing the palest pastel colours and laces. It suggests a more calm lifestyle and a feeling of elegance.

The December 1984 issue of Vogue *was in praise of "the Englishwoman," for which a photograph by Lord Snowdon was chosen of the Princess in this ivory satin dress to typify "the world's best-known and most romantic example, the Princess of Wales."*

Photographer: Lord Snowdon/Camera Press

White Abraham silk ottoman bustier dress with petal sleeves.

Vogue, April 1986: "New Luminaries . . . a Puff for Summer Parties."

This dress "hovers around the body." The arum lily sleeves frame the shoulders, and the bodice points into a finely gathered ankle-length skirt.

Photographer: Paolo Roversi / The Condé Nast Publications Ltd

The Chelsea Design Company 1982–88

HOVERING AROUND THE BODY

There followed five years of chaos and many firsts for me. Following the orders for maternity clothes throughout the Princess' first pregnancy, I was not expecting to hear from her until she was pregnant again. I was therefore astonished in the autumn of 1982 to receive a telephone call from her lady-in-waiting telling me that the Princess wanted me to suggest some designs for coats for her formal engagements. After the initial thrill I realised that I knew nothing about tailoring at all. So we literally looked in the Yellow Pages. Apart from the skill we required, we needed to find someone with discretion. After asking a few questions about the kind of work they did, we asked them for the names of some of their best clients to see if they would divulge this easily. We confined our search to those who refused to answer this last question. I don't know if it was luck but after only two days I found a wonderful tailor on the third floor in South Molton Street. Anthony was totally eccentric and despite nearing retirement age he was completely unset in his ways, which was just as well because I think he thought I was mad. However, I knew exactly what I wanted, he never questioned it, and within a few weeks I had it: a long-line fitted coat with defined shoulder in a traditional military style, a mix of French cut and English sentiment. These were new skills that were not within my repertoire of dressmaking as they involved firmer fabrics and a different internal con-

Red barathea wool double-breasted coat with a half-back belt in black velvet.

Commissioned by HRH The Princess of Wales. Visit to Chamwood Mencap, Loughborough, 22 March 1984.

The Princess first wore this coat to open a children's playground in Kennington, Southeast London, in December 1982, but this picture shows her wearing it two years later. It's one of my favourite pictures because it was not often the Princess is pictured next to someone taller than she is, and this very tall Lord Lieutenant makes an elegant contrast in matching colours. The coat itself is my first tailored piece, and, unknown to me at the time, was the start of a long love affair between me and couture tailoring.

Photographer: Tim Graham
Hat by Frederick Fox

SPRING/SUMMER COLLECTION 1984

**Catherine Walker wearing a camel cash-
mere single-breasted coat with chocolate
velvet collar.**

*This photograph was used for one of our first
advertising campaigns. In it I wear a full-length
coat with the same neat shoulder and fluid silhouette that is shown on page 25 as commissioned by
the Princess of Wales.*

Photograph by The Chelsea Design Co.

struction. I didn't know it at the time but
this was the beginning of a long love affair
between me and tailoring and of course a
long professional relationship and friendship
with the Princess of Wales.

I was still hovering around the body.
Instead of a collection I would produce a
continuous flow of new projects throughout
each season. These were not "designs" in the
art-school meaning of the word but the next
technical venture that I could explore. I had
not yet perceived the body as a whole. I was
hovering like a busy bee around the body,
darting this way and that, playing with a
lapel, a drop waist, a sleeve, a bias cut. Mixed
in with all this I now had the added challenge
of undertaking individual commissions for
HRH the Princess of Wales, which I saw prin-
cipally as new technical fields to explore. I
was extremely moved by the idea of making
clothes for the Princess of Wales. But what
really absorbed me was the technical adventure and all the angles of the body that were
opening up to me through her patronage.
Whenever I opened a newspaper and saw my
work, it was not a lapel or a sleeve that I saw,
but a whole body. I had buried myself in my
work after John's death but now I was having
to step back a little.

In the showroom we were very busy
indeed, and I was still doing most of the selling, although I was not in the least motivated
by financial or personal gain. I was completely
motivated by my creative work though Saïd
was firmly nudging me to prevent my straying
too far off the commercial rails. It was at this
time that he appointed our first public rela-
tions firm to *avoid* publicity! Journalists could
not understand my motives and were puzzled
and a little disappointed by my disregard for

publicity associated with the Princess of Wales. Otherwise my relationship with the press was warm: Hamish Bowles, Debbie Mason, Anna Harvey, Vanessa de Lisle, Liz Walker, and Suzy Menkes were all genuinely interested in my work, and I relished working with them on one-off commissions for their editorial pieces and general editorial work through the offices of our PR consultant, Phyllis Walters.

In the early years of the company the staff had been all-rounders because the business was simply not large enough to sustain specialists. By 1983, however, we had developed enough commercially, and I had grown enough technically, that we could engage our first star pattern cutter, our first star machinist, our first professional sales assistant, and our first tambour beader.

I know it sounds ridiculous but this was when I first noticed my competitors. Anyone else who has ever run a business would be aware of their competitors from the marketplace. To me the marketplace might just as well have been on the moon and my first awareness of fellow designers came via my new staff. These professionals had all worked with other designers, and whether I liked it or not I found I was being compared. Despite this unexpected appraisal it was a pure joy to have these skilled craftsmen and craftswomen around me. You know you have the best because *they* nag *you*. All the time I was stretching to the limit and it was a blessing to be nagged because I could stop nagging myself and grow in another direction. On a personal level, despite all the problems new to me but no doubt well-known to all other employers, I grew to love these technicians and professionals and they

became my extended family. And all the while, as I was selling, fitting, making, and trying to administer all these professional people, I was little by little being forced to reopen myself to the outside world.

In 1985 I came across a book by the photographer John French. He was an Englishman born in London in 1907. His photographic work was widely known and respected in the world of post-war fashion. What struck me about him was the clarity of his work and how his photographs captured the femininity and elongation of the body. In fact he used to say to his models, "feel as though you have a string which comes out through a hole in the top of your head and is attached to the ceiling." At the same time, I met George, who I believe to this day is the best tailor in England and probably far beyond. I had realised that the precision I wanted for my new jackets and coats could only be achieved by men's tailors. However most men's tailors have a touch that is a little too heavy for the fluidity of the female shape. George had a precision and lightness of touch that could have been part of John French's images.

This was the beginning of my handwriting. I suddenly discovered the *midriff* and that I could elongate the torso through the structured approach of tailoring. I could take a step back and create a silhouette that did not rely so much on the body inside it. Suddenly everything became clear, and I realised that everything I was going to *design* from now on would have to do with elongation. Once I had grasped this it was obvious to me that this was going to lead to the sensuality of fluid shapes. I saw it as the way a man can't resist grasping a woman at the waist. Straight away I stopped playing with unconnected details and design-

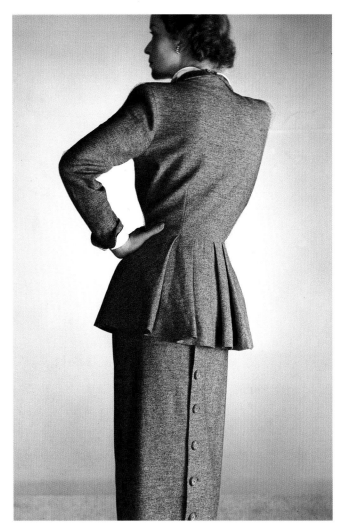

1949 suit by Wolsey,
photographed by John French.

The work of John French proved to be an enormous influence in my early work. I recall coming across a book in 1985 in which he was quoted as asking his models "to feel as though you have a string which comes out through a hole on the top of your head and is attached to the ceiling." John French's models walked tall and left an image that remained in the forefront of my mind thereafter. It made me aware of the importance and beauty of elongating the torso.

Photograph by V & A Picture Library

ing "half-garments" that denied me the whole silhouette. The *hovering* was over and the *designing* had begun.

If, before this time, I had felt I was working hard, it was nothing compared to how I now started to push myself. What had begun as a kind of therapy had now developed into a passion. I was noticing the fashion world for the first time because I could connect with it. As a late starter I had so much catching up to do that even while travelling around the corner to local London suppliers I found myself reading everything I could lay my hands on about fashion from newspapers and magazines to glossy hardbacks. Everywhere I saw midriff: Piquet, Schiaparelli, Mainbocher, Molyneaux, and St. Laurent. I saw midriff in Hollywood: Marlene Dietrich, Lauren Bacall, Katherine Hepburn, and Kay Francis. It was a consuming passion—no music, no reading, no television, no social life, no exercise I'm afraid, and no pampering myself. I was either with clients or with the production room or thinking about midriff.

I was not thinking of shows, collections, focus, impact, or even handwriting. Instead I was marvelling at the different weights and textures of fabrics and how, with different interlinings, I could make them do completely different things: how I could use a dress block (the flat pattern for a basic body shape) to create a jacket block; how the jacket will then curve around the body like a dress and how I could reverse the exercise. Conversely, using a traditional jacket block I could produce a dress that would skim the body.

I remember Barrie, my first star pattern cutter, fitting a dress on me (I used to try on all the new designs). The closeness of her touching surprised me. I was learning about tenderness and intimacy with the female shape, both of which are such an essential part of my designing. In the years to follow, until I became ill, I sized every client who ordered a new shape, taking time to focus on the stretch and elongation of their bodies.

My doctorate had been about Edwin Panowski and iconology and I understood designing to be the development of one's own language. Fashion shows have a mirror effect that reflects the language of the designer through the reaction of others and the print of the press. As I did not hold shows (because I did not wholesale), I did not have the benefit of this feedback and I used to write myself new design briefs every season without knowing why I was doing it, but of course it was for that very reason.

I was also learning that clothes were not just a physical silhouette, they also have to move you emotionally. I started to notice colours properly again for the first time in five years. When I was a little girl I used to spend my summer holidays on the Normandy beaches, the colours of which are part of me—the greys, blues, beiges, and pinks, which on a cloudy day are soft and moody but on a bright day are the clearest, palest colours. They produce the most touching light watercolours. In my new world the concept of colours and light led straight to embroidery. I was again like a child who had discovered a new bag of sweets, but again I did not start with design dreams but by asking, "how is it done?"

In France there are wonderful embroidery houses which are designers in their own right. The French couture shows are a spectacle of embroidery and it follows that there is a strong infrastructure to support this demand. In England the demand is less, and as a result, the embroidery companies work more like an in-house embroiderer—the design input comes primarily from the designer rather than the embroiderer. It is demanding but extremely rewarding. I have developed a particularly good relationship with the very skillful London embroiderers S. Lock Ltd., with whom I have worked since 1989. As I do not hold a show, my embroidery is concerned with close-up work rather than the distant impact of a catwalk. I am also particularly fond of three-dimensional tactile work rather than the flatter story-telling embroidery.

My designs were now pushing the limit of the infrastructure offered in London and soon I started to venture outside Sydney Street in search of handmade buttons and intricate passementerie, sumptuous feathers, and later, sharp continental hats. Inevitably the trail led full circle back to France, where the whole thing had started and where I had left John.

Pinstriped coatdress in white Corisia wool.

Commissioned by HRH The Princess Of Wales. Official visit to La Spezia, Italy, May 1985.

When I was asked to prepare a number of designs for the Princess's tour of Italy in March 1985, she chose this coatdress which I suggested in a white pinstripe wool. I did not realise she intended to wear it at La Spezia, where, together with Graham Smith's perky sailor hat, it perfectly suited the background of this northern Italian naval port. The line of the tailored shoulder follows the natural shoulderline of the body, and the sleeve is precise and clean. The sharp tailoring was a move away from the soft tailoring that had been prevalent in England in the 1980s.

Photographer: Tim Graham

Dove grey Corisia silk douppion tailcoat and white linen shift.

Commissioned by HRH The Princess of Wales. Royal Ascot, Ladies' Day, June 1988.

The Daily Mail, 17 June 1988: "The Princess wins, hats or tails."

Weddings, garden parties, and Ascot have always been occasions to dress up, and I thought this particularly English habit was an opportunity for the Princess to wear something that took the habit to new heights. This suit was designed to emulate the traditional cutaway tailcoat that was very commonly worn by gentlemen during the Regency period of George III. It was a challenge to execute sharp men's tailoring with fabrics such as this fine silk douppion, using a dress block to give the coat a more curvaceous line.

Photograph by Photographers International

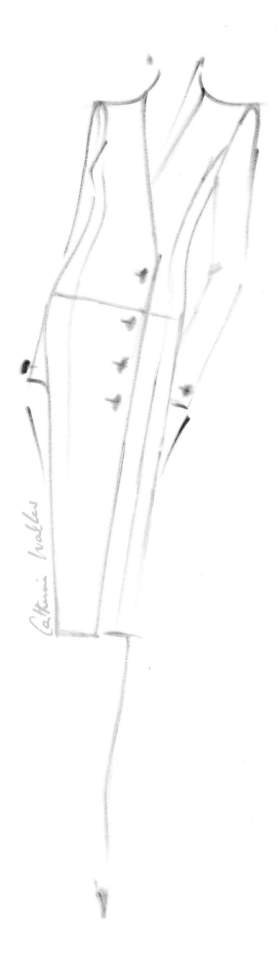

opposite:

Pink and red trompe l'oeil coatdress.

Commissioned by HRH The Princess Of Wales for a state visit to Dubai, United Arab Emirates, March 1989.

The play of pink and red colours creates a trompe l'oeil effect that emphasizes the low waist. The balance of the flat buttons reflects the minimalist feeling of the design in Taroni silk douppion. The colours pink, red, and gold were inspired by images of the vegetable-dyed traditional colours of the bedouin. We felt they played beautifully against the heat of the Arabian sands.

The long sleeve, modest neckline, and longer length skirt of this coatdress were chosen out of respect to the country for which it was designed, where women dress with modesty. In choosing this length of skirt for the state visit, the Princess was reverting to the length she adopted when she first joined the royal family. Over the years the Princess's skirt lengths had been a busy topic for fashion journalists. It is true that they went up and down, and in my memory they are a little like a barometer that altered to reflect her changing life. At the time of her divorce they lengthened; shortly before her death they were probably shortest. I always liked the fact that she didn't follow fashion but did what was right for her.

Photographer: Jayne Fincher / Photographers International
Hat by Philip Somerville

Scarlet and purple Taroni silk douppion suit with yellow crepe drap T-shirt.

Commissioned by HRH The Princess of Wales for a state visit to Hong Kong, November 1989.

I made various sketch proposals for the Princess's forthcoming tour to Hong Kong, but we were unable to meet because she was in Scotland for the summer. So she sent a note from Balmoral via Anne Beckwith-Smith, her lady-in-waiting, giving me a few pointers on how to proceed. After further discussion, we developed one design that used the colours of the silks to echo the exotic Chinese setting. The wide belt emphasizes the waist and elongates the body. The pagoda-shaped hat is by Philip Somerville.

The Daily Mail, 8 November 1989:

"Princess Diana sailed into the lion's den of Hong Kong last night and caused an oriental sensation.

"In a stunning outfit of flaming reds, violet, and yellow, completed by a Chinese-style hat, she turned the authorities' fear of protests spectacularly on its head. If there were any demonstrators they were drowned out by the sheer joy of a welcome that echoed clear across the harbour to the twinkling lights of Kowloon. Ten thousand people, crushed into pens along Queen's Pier, cheered as Diana glided with Prince Charles into downtown Hong Kong in an old launch.

"One hand checked the hat with its purple silk crown which the breeze tried to dislodge. With her other hand, held away from her Catherine Walker silk bolero suit, she reached out at a stay to steady herself. Then her arm went up, and lifting her head to reveal a face full of smiles, she waved a greeting of her own. The effect was staggering."

Photographer: Dave Chancellor / Alpha

AUTUMN/WINTER COLLECTION 1986/87

Navy Prince of Wales check double-breasted city suit with extended length jacket and low slung buttons.

Vogue, February 1987: "The Short Sharp Prince of Wales Suit."

Cecilia Chancellor wears a classic proportion double-breasted city suit reworked to a longer jacket and shorter skirt. This proportion became typical of our collections in the late eighties.

In the early nineties we were approached by an airline to design the uniform for their cabin crew, and we felt this type of design would translate well into a uniform. This was the opposite extreme to couture. Unfortunately, they found our ways too idiosyncratic to fit into the tight world of corporate clothing, and the project never took off.

Photographer: Terence Donovan / The Condé Nast Publications Ltd.

SPRING/SUMMER COLLECTION 1985

Fitted jacket and tail skirt in golden yellow glazed chintz.

Harpers & Queen, May 1985: "Sing Something Simple."

By the mid-eighties the Princess of Wales had become a focal point of reference for British society at events such as Ascot, and Harpers & Queen *selected this outfit as a suitable example for such an occasion: "following the lead of a certain Princess of Wales the search is on for the outfit striking the smartest note of the season."*

Photographer: Barry Dunn

Chintz by Arthur Sanderson and Sons Ltd., London

opposite:

AUTUMN/WINTER COLLECTION 1987/88

**Curved pocket jacket
in scarlet barathea wool
modelled by Yasmin Le Bon.**

Cover, British *Vogue*, August 1987.

The curved block of an evening-dress pattern has been translated into tailoring. The hipline is emphasized by the continuation of the seamline through the pocket. The curvaceous shape, with its pronounced shoulder, was typical of 1980s "power dressing" and I used the width of the pocket to balance the width of the shoulders. The collarless jacket was a favourite of mine right through into the nineties, and I enjoyed wearing them myself because there was no weight around the neck. Above all, I loved the simplicity and the femininity of the longer neck and the emphasis it gives to the face.

Photographer: Patrick Demarchelier / The Condé Nast Publications Ltd.

AUTUMN/WINTER COLLECTION 1987/88

Scarlet Buche silk velvet military jacket.

Harpers & Queen, September 1989: "A Study in Scarlet."

This pattern is cut to a high waist over a high-waisted midcalf skirt. Ansiline gold buttons create the plastron effect. The traditional English colour of red for formal military jackets is softened by the use of silk velvet, which is a challenge to tailor to a precise shape but gives the jacket a sense of femininity.

Photographer: Marie Laure de Decker / The National Magazine Co. Ltd.

Opposite:

AUTUMN/WINTER COLLECTION 1987/88

Red Dormeuil barathea wool cropped military jacket.

Vogue, November 1987: "Military Coup: Winter Uniforms."

"The decorated, decorative modern hussar strides forth in new uniforms. The look is all about powerful shape, solid colour, brilliant embellishment, and a sense of adventure."
   Naomi Campbell parades this military jacket. The proportion of the eighties shoulderline over the high-waisted jersey leggings emphasizes the elongation of the torso. The graduated military buttons punctuate the extension of the body.

Photographer: Hans Feurer / The Condé Nast Publications Ltd.

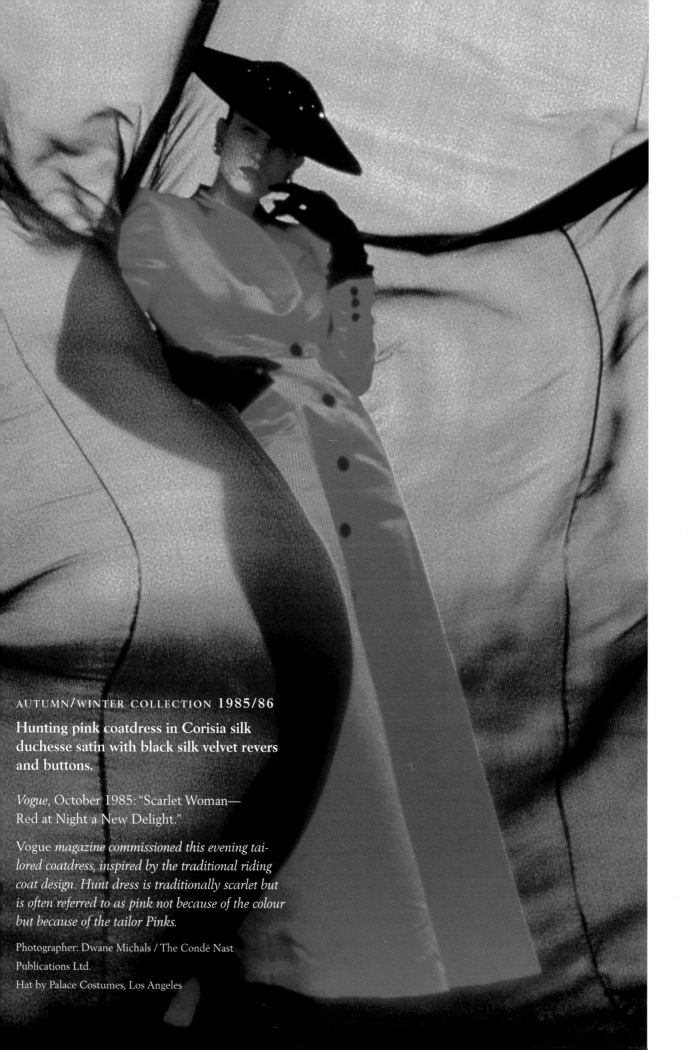

AUTUMN/WINTER COLLECTION 1985/86

Hunting pink coatdress in Corisia silk duchesse satin with black silk velvet revers and buttons.

Vogue, October 1985: "Scarlet Woman—Red at Night a New Delight."

Vogue *magazine commissioned this evening tailored coatdress, inspired by the traditional riding coat design. Hunt dress is traditionally scarlet but is often referred to as pink not because of the colour but because of the tailor Pinks.*

Photographer: Dwane Michals / The Condé Nast Publications Ltd.

Hat by Palace Costumes, Los Angeles

above

AUTUMN/WINTER COLLECTION **1988/89**

Midnight blue and claret silk velvet column dress with train.

This picture of Catherine Bailey was taken by Horst during the Makers of Photographic History symposium hosted by Bradford's National Museum of Photography to commemorate 150 years of photography. My intention to stretch the torso with my designs is typified in these two photographs and the photograph on the book's cover, each of which show the fluid elongation of the body.

Photographer: Horst P. Horst / The Condé Nast Publications Ltd.
Hat by Stephen Jones

left

AUTUMN/WINTER COLLECTION **1988/89**

Acid lemon and black Buche silk evening dress.

Vogue, April 1990: "Yellow and Black."

Catherine Bailey wears this tailored evening dress with Elizabethan neckline. The high bodice and long column split skirt work well together to elongate the body.

Photographer: David Bailey / The Condé Nast Publications Ltd.

Lilac Clerici crepe dress with English stitchwork embroidery in chenilles and silks.

Commissioned by HRH The Princess of Wales for a state visit to the United Arab Emirates, March 1989.

My experience of embroidery in 1989 was negligible, so I was both anxious and thrilled by this first piece of embroidery commissioned by the Princess. At this time the Princess was emerging as a major figure on the international stage and I saw this as an opportunity to create something traditional rather than avant garde. I wanted to capture the English country garden colouring for a young princess while at the same time work on a base colour that was fitting for the Gulf States. After about a week of deliberation I chose this soft amethyst colour because it had both the lilac freshness of a spring garden and a hint of the mystery of the East.

After many trial pieces of handwork, the graphics and colours were developed with the embroiderers, S. Lock Ltd., in London, who finally completed the work in traditional stitchwork and beads. The dress was originally worn for a state visit to the United Arab Emirates in March 1989 and had a full skirt. It was recut to a straight silhouette for the state visit to Korea in November 1992.

Both dresses were high waisted with a tailored top in Buche lilac silk. Roses were the obvious choice for the embroidered motif, being a symbol of the country the Princess was representing. The roses are not seen "flat-on" but "tilted" to re-create the way a natural flower would catch the light. The use of embroidered symbols on royal clothes has a long heritage. HM The Queen's Coronation dress by Hartnell featured the flower emblems of all the dominions of which she was to be sovereign.

Photographers: David Hartley / REX Features,
Stephen Hayward (detail)

Grand tailcoat in burgundy Bouton Renaud silk velvet with imperial gold stitchwork flower motifs and pearl embroidery over a burgundy silk velvet full-length bustier dress.

Commissioned by HRH The Princess of Wales and worn to the London film premiere of *Steel Magnolias* in aid of The Prince's Trust, February 1990.

After ten years of designing for the Princess I was well aware of the fact that she was photographed from every conceivable angle. The embroidery around the nape of the neck and back vents emphasizes the femininity of the silhouette. The cutaway shape of the jacket elongates the waist and adds formality to the design.

This design was in fact inspired by the colouring of an Imperial Russian court dress and was originally offered to the Princess as a burgundy tailcoat over a rich ivory silk crepe bustier dress. The Princess, however, felt that all burgundy would be more fluid and easier to wear, and I think she was right.

Photographer: Tim Graham

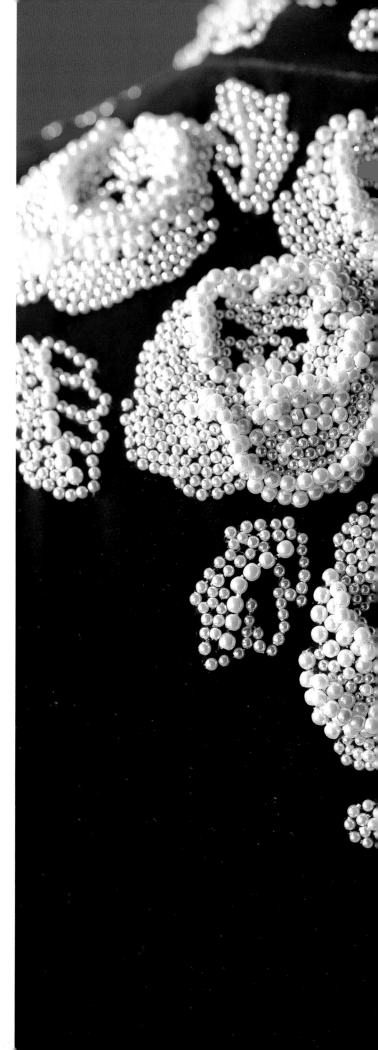

AUTUMN/WINTER COLLECTION 1991/92

High-necked tailcoat in Buche maroon silk velvet.

The embroidered plastron gives a military quality that contrasts with the femininity of the pearl guipure flowers. The overall effect of this collection piece is more masculine than the tailcoat commissioned by the Princess of Wales.

Photographer: Stephen Hayward

Catherine Walker

Ruched dress in pink and indigo warp-printed silk taffeta.

Commissioned by HRH The Princess of Wales for an official visit to Melbourne, January 1988.

Warp printing is a dying art but it is still practised in Lyon. The fibres of the warp are held on a bed and printed before they are made into a fabric by weaving with the unprinted weft. The result is a hazy, almost impressionist effect. The ruching of the dress emphasizes the blurring of the flowers, and the warp taffeta pattern lends itself beautifully to the ruching effect. The modern slashed leg contrasts with the antiquity of the material. The colours indigo and pink were chosen for an English Princess to wear for an Australian summer.

The dress is perhaps most famous for the occasion when the Princess and HRH The Prince of Wales led the dancing at the Bicentennial Dinner Dance in Melbourne to the strains of Glen Miller's "In the Mood."

Photographers: Brendan Beirne / REX Features, Stephen Hayward (detail)

Asymmetric dress with re-embroidered flowers on ivory romain satin by Clerici.

Commissioned by HRH The Princess of Wales. Official visit to Brazil in 1991.

The warp taffeta effect is re-created in embroidery when the flat sequins and bugle beads are displaced to imitate the effect of the warp and weft of the fabric. The softness of the colours imitates the faded feeling of antique fabrics and contrasts with the sharp asymmetry of the design.

The Princess of Wales took great care to honour the traditions and feelings of each country that she visited. Shortly before this visit to Brazil, the national football team had lost to Argentina in the World Cup and the country was depressed about this disaster. We received instructions that in view of these circumstances we should not design anything in green, yellow, and blue, which were the official colours of the team, and definitely not in blue and white, which were the colours of the Argentinian football team.

Photographers: Tim Graham, Stephen Hayward (detail)

Asymmetric dress in black and white.

Commissioned by HRH The Princess of Wales. Premiere of Steven Spielberg's *Hook* at the Odeon, Leicester Square, in aid of the Hospital for Sick Children, Great Ormond Street, April 1992.

The bodice of this dress was embroidered in ribbon lace and scattered pearls with a pearl border. The ribbon is applied using a Cornely machine and attached with a chain stitch onto the fabric of the dress. Its application is entirely freehand and when finished produces a curly effect similar to astrakhan.
We made a replica of this dress for Madame Tussauds in 1997 to replace the state dress that I made for the Princess in 1989 that was previously on display.

A Couturier In London
1988–97

As my work focussed more on the tailored silhouette with the elongated midriff and sharp shoulderline as worn by the Princess of Wales, the press began to label me as a *tailor* rather than as a *dressmaker*. But this was actually only part of the story. I am very French and hence favour structured and formal clothes. French women seem to follow a more rigid code. In the mid-sixties I had come to England attracted by its quirkiness and freedom and I liked the fact that English women were individual and eccentric in their way of dress. But later on what I really liked about England was not its quirkiness but its airiness, coolness, and lightness, which in terms of clothes I call "flattery." It is as if some of the reserve of the older couturiers like Dior were still part of the English spirit, something to do with a feeling of having time and space to relish the sensuality of clothes which is so alien to the rush and brouhaha of the current couture shows.

There is to the French mind a unique English aristocratic charm that translates itself into fashion as the very palest ivory, icy blues, dove grey, soft pinks, and *eau de nil*, an absence of fussiness and shapes with no extra bits or decoration unnecessarily added. There is also something to do with the textures and small nuances rather than the richer, bolder play of continental shapes and colours—a discreet sensuality rather than an up-front sexuality. After twenty years in London I had become very aware of English influences, and both French and English traditions were important to my work.

With these feelings at heart, a penchant for technical know-how, the patronage of HRH The Princess of Wales and other loyal clients, and the support of Liz Tilberis (then the editor of British *Vogue*) my work developed inevitably towards couture. In the 1980s few English designers were interested in couture. Even the traditional couture techniques of Savile Row were being passed over in favour of soft tailoring. As many English designers either packed up or moved to France I felt determined to make a couture house in Britain and anchor my work in London.

The French Chambre de Syndicale has rigid rules about allowing a company to be called a house of couture. I never tried to belong within such a formal arrangement. I just developed my own way of doing things and I did it throughout with a hands-on approach. I now find that my company is formed along the lines of a traditional couture house with separate rooms for tailoring, flou, and embroidery. However, my real intention was just to design beautifully crafted clothes for the joy of the women who were going to wear them.

Although the first couturier, Frederick Worth, was an Englishman, the heart of couture has always been in France. To produce couture clothes in England one has to create one's own infrastructure of specialist crafts. I would repeatedly visit suppliers in Paris, and these visits were rejuvenating. I would hold long and detailed conversations with Parisian taxi drivers about *passementerie* (a kind of corded embroidery). When I visited a button designer, I would hear the words "beauty," "love," "poetry"—about buttons. I would return to London in a buoyant mood but always even more aware that what I was trying to do in England was rather crazy. It was so much effort to create something beautiful with very little support. I was perpetually forcing the development of the studio with the only means available to me—my emotions and my physical strength. Despite this the technical growth and achievement of my team continued to thrill and surprise me as I gathered together some of the most talented people in their crafts.

In the early days these positions were filled by the lovely people I have described earlier. They were the gifted part-timers. As the years passed I started to attract the professionals of the industry. As many designers in the UK sadly closed their businesses during the recession years of the early nineties I was often asked to find a "home" for their most precious employees and I can think of at least eight examples. The couture world in England is a very small world indeed, and I had seen the names of the same pattern cutters, sample cutters, tailors, and sample machinists over and over again, and I was able to pick the best. Like any industry I am sure the most talented people are full of idiosyncrasies.

The tailors are a charming group who tend to work alone in their own studios. They are mostly men, prone to being "artistic" and doing things their own way. Each tailor has his or her own "handle" or touch so their output varies in size, general appearance, and can even result in samples made inside out (although one such example was a bestseller). They can have little regard for delivery times which causes endless confusion with the showroom. These lovely people, who would be crushed by a factory system,

thrive in the freedom of individual expression and the search for the cleanest shoulder and the perfectly hung sleeve. One just has to appreciate that "handmade" means slightly different each time.

George, my sample tailor, lives on the Oxford/Northamptonshire border so I rarely see him. In fact, in twelve years I think I have met him less than twelve times. But we have developed such a strong working relationship that we can create the most intricate tailored designs over the telephone. We work on identical stands. I send him detailed toiles with copious notes and then telephone him to discuss moving seams up and down or left and right an eighth of an inch. It is such a joy to receive a box containing the perfect jacket, as if he had not even touched it. Many of the tailored designs seen on the Princess during a period of thirteen years were made by George. It was such a pleasure to see them on the world stage, particularly in the early days when nobody knew about my existence and I could just enjoy them in private.

Because George lived some distance away, the sheer logistics of sending, discussing, cutting, making, and returning hundreds of individually tailored suits and tailored evening dresses were themselves a design problem. This was mostly solved using a Red Star delivery service via Paddington. However, to maintain an occasional face-to-face contact, Saïd and George used to meet halfway. To make it worthwhile, other goods such as dress stands and rolls of fabric were taken to George to exchange at the same time. The halfway point was agreed as Junction 6 on the M40 and at the due time he and Saïd would meet on a secluded slip road and reverse their cars into a tail to tail position. George is a man of few words and so after shaking hands and a few moments of pleasantries they would open their boots and swap what must have looked like very suspicious human-shaped packages before driving off in the directions from which they had come.

Unlike the tailors the *petites mains* are mainly women who on the whole work in our own studios. The studios are divided into little rooms because with so many talented individuals, a "hothouse" atmosphere can develop. These professionals are dressmakers in their own right but work in our team for the specialist talents for which they each have a gift—for example, the perfect drape, the lightest chiffon touch, the smoothest velvet seams, and the finest rouleaux. They are waited on by a group of solid no-nonsense technicians as their time is too precious to waste with nothing to do. Without the buffer of the licensing, everything we do must pay for itself. Although there is a spirit of cooperation among these talented women there are many "flashpoint" areas. Most clients will be unaware that the *inside* of their cocktail dress is controversial. It is almost impossible to ask one sampler to finish another sampler's work in an emergency, because they will inevitably disagree about how the dress should have been crafted from the outset.

My experience of cutters is that they seem to fall into two very different character groups. The pattern cutters are technicians who take the concept of a design into the reality of a pattern. Because of their proximity to the designer, they tend to be emotional, sensitive, and therefore rather temperamen-tal. The other cutters are sample cutters, who are very stable individuals and who spend hours each day delicately cutting thousands of pounds' worth of luxury fabrics into intricate shapes.

My greatest deviation from traditional French couture was that although I invited my clients to view the collection twice yearly, I did not present a show. This soon became a real problem with the fashion press and made me an outsider to the fashion system. There has been some severe pressure on me to conform to the "circus" and I perfectly understood why. I was dressing the Princess of Wales and could have been a great performer in that circus. I knew instinctively however that if I ventured into licensing or diffusion lines, I would lose control of my couture work.

In 1994 I was interviewed by a senior fashion journalist who demanded to know why I did not present a show. When I replied that it was because I only wanted to sell my designs and not perfume, I don't think she had any idea what I was talking about. The "new" couturier has the prescribed job of presenting a collection with an extravagance that places the label in the public consciousness in order to sell that public licenced goods. I have always seen my work as confined to my clients and my atelier, and because I own my company, I can decide whether I want to concentrate on couture or use couture to augment profits on licenced goods.

My clients tend to be strong women who have a public role to play: lawyers, business or media people, film stars, aristocracy, and royalty. It is not only that these women need to dress up—they also seem to share an attitude of mind, they hold themselves straight and have to look tall and effortlessly self-assured. I would so enjoy taking every fitting with each client in the showroom—making each woman tall and beautiful. I relished the complicity and trust that developed between us. For me couture clothes are a gesture of love to my clients.

The burden of swimming against the changing tide of couture was daunting. Sometimes it was difficult even to find the time to dream. I should have learned to deputise but I was designing, running the showroom, dealing with the growing production and, unknown to me at the time, my body could not cope with the strain. In April 1995 I found I had breast cancer.

Breast Cancer

I had in fact been feeling rather unwell for more than a year and it had even crossed my mind that I may have had a serious illness. At times I felt a distortion as though part of my body wanted to go forward and another part of my body wanted to go backward. After a certain age every woman thinks of menopause, and it occurred to me that a sudden onset could have been the cause of my symptoms so I visited my gynaecologist to ask for his help. We talked about Hormone Replacement Therapy, and I expressed my reservations because of my known sensitivity to any drugs. I had showed him a small lump in my breast and he said it was nothing.

The HRT made me nauseous and at the same time so energetic that I could not sleep. My nerves became taught. I understood that this was an unusual reaction, but after several visits to my gynaecologist it seemed that he

could make no new suggestions. In my own search for an answer I read everything I could on menopause. I eventually learned about *natural* progesterone, which was unavailable in England at the time, but which I eventually found I could obtain in France. I did, and overnight there was a considerable improvement. I could feel my true self coming to life again. I was ready to put this year-long nightmare behind me when I found that the lump in my breast had grown.

Things moved very quickly. Within three days the result of a biopsy was telephoned through to my husband. It was a normal busy Monday morning and as usual things were hectic in my office. I looked up to see Saïd walk into my office and I could see from his face that I had cancer. Although it was not a medical certainty at that time, I knew. At that instant everything slowed down in my mind, and normal time no longer existed. I started to anticipate the inevitable change of pace to which I would have to succumb. I went to the showroom for an appointment with a client and I remember I hugged a baby. The showroom was crowded but I felt a terrible loneliness and the same sick feeling in the stomach that I remember after John's death. The noise of the showroom sounded distant, and I contemplated in my own silence the braveness that I knew I was going to have to find in myself.

I went to the hospital for the lumpectomy the following day. It was a sunny spring morning. Strangely, I felt a temporary sense of relief, that I could give my body into the care of professionals and would no longer have to search so hard to find the answers. What I did not know was that I was going to be faced with a completely new set of questions and a much greater and more radical change to my life.

A week later I moved to a new studio, which Saïd had speedily made ready for me away from the turmoil of the showroom. There I could rest in complete solitude but still be near the work I loved. In the weeks that followed I began radiotherapy treatment, and I began to consider a new way to work. My days used to be very long, and I would meet perhaps up to fifty people a day. I now came to rely on one assistant to relay messages to different parts of the business and carry sheafs of written instructions to everybody. I made no appointments with clients or the press.

I was so shocked that something I loved so much had made me so ill that at times I felt like running away from it all. Little by little, however, I was overwhelmed by the love of not only of my family and friends but loyal staff and dear clients whose daily messages, gifts, and offers of hospitality were in themselves an uplifting experience. It seems that amidst the chaos of my work before my illness, I had focussed on the hurt that is the penalty of success and overlooked the genuine love all around me.

Once again I started reading, this time not about menopause but about breast cancer. But the more I read the more I believed that my menopause and breast cancer were linked. I had started to find acupuncture extremely beneficial and through my reading I formed my own regime of diet, meditation, and exercise. My body, which had become so unbalanced during the preceding few years, gradually started to stabilise, and in the weeks of quiet solitude and reflection I think I understood my body for the first time.

My work has started to swing back into position. I have more space and freedom to dream, to experiment with ideas and shapes, to create a garment again for the sheer pleasure of wondering how it works. My relationship with clients is lighter and more affectionate. I am profoundly touched by the support and loyalty they have given me and want to return this with the gift of making them clothes that convey a sense of space and freedom in their lives. The cancer has given me a chance to take a deep breath, a pause. I had spent my life until now apologising for the sensitivity of my body, believing that it was my body that was in the wrong. The sensitivity has meant that I suffered much from the setbacks of my life—my parents' divorce, widowhood, cancer, and more lately Diana's death—but I now know that the same sensitivity is not a cause for regret, for the awareness and insight have enriched me, and for the first time I am walking tall.

August 1997

Reading List

Carper, Jean. *Food: Your Miracle Medicine*. London: Simon & Schuster Ltd., 1995.

Dalton, Katharina. *Once a Month*. 5th ed. London: Fontana, 1991.

Diamond, W. John, W. Lee Cowden, and Burton Goldberg. *Definitive Guide to Cancer*. Tiburon, CA: Future Medicine Publishing, 1991.

Erasmus, Udo. *Fats That Heal, Fats That Kill*. Burnaby, British Columbia: Alive Books, 1993.

Hanh, Thich Nhat, *Peace is Every Step*. London: Bantam Books, 1995.

Lee, John R. *What Your Doctor May Not Tell You about Menopause*. New York: Warner Books, 1996.

Read, Cathy. *Preventing Breast Cancer*. London: Pandora, 1995.

Salamon, Maureen Kennedy. *Nutrition: The Cancer Answer 2*. Mountain View, CA: Statford Publishing, 1996.

Diana,
Princess of Wales

On the day of Lady Diana Spencer's wedding I was on holiday on Lake Como with Saïd and the girls. Together with the guests at the villa where we were staying, we sat transfixed by the ceremony on television. I was captivated by the extraordinary ritual in which this teenage girl entered the cathedral and re-emerged a Princess. I was entranced by the transformation that had taken place and moved to wish it had been me who had made the dress, as I am sure everyone else in my profession did.

Of course that was absurd, as my knowledge of designing was in its infancy, and I was therefore astonished by the request that came four months later in November 1981. It was my first commission from the Princess, who wanted some maternity dresses. It was the start of a relationship that lasted almost sixteen years. Had she lived, my last order would have been delivered to her almost sixteen years to the day I am writing this, in November 1997.

I remember standing outside the shop in the rain after the first order had been delivered and thinking "I wonder where *this* is going to lead." My career had only just begun, and I was very aware of how little I knew about couture. However, I was also aware that the Princess, so young and pretty, did not need Paris straight away—it would have overwhelmed her.

I recall our first meeting. It was a wintry February morning at Sydney Street. Anne Beckwith-Smith, the Princess's lady-in-waiting, had telephoned me to ask if it would be convenient for the Princess to pay us a visit within the hour. A few minutes later, before we had time to become nervous, she walked in wearing one of my designs in pistachio green wool. The visit, on the face of it, was to thank me for the care I had taken in making her maternity dresses. But when she arrived, I immediately sensed that it was in fact to take a discreet look at me and where I worked. For my part, I was struck by her complexion, which was more pale, fragile, and clear than her photographs showed. Her eyes were disarming and bright blue under a half fringe. It was a touching meeting because we both wanted to be warm to each other but our shyness kept us apart. We weren't without our similarities. We were both tall (the same height of five feet, ten inches) both shy, both coming to terms with a new career, and, unknown to me at the time, we shared the same starsign, Cancer, and we had both seen our parents divorce in early childhood.

Designing for the Princess was an extraordinary opportunity. It was about beauty and dreams, and I took it on with enormous spirit. I was looking for an opportunity to put my heart back in place. I was still adjusting to widowhood but wanted and felt ready to give two hundred percent, and the Princess needed that.

I think what surprised me most during this early period were two things: the Princess's ease and modesty, and the fact that despite the guidance she was given, nothing could really be enough for the awesome situation she was faced with. It was obvious that she needed a carefully thought-out formality considering the situation and the momentousness of the responsibility.

She was so easy, and her reaction to a drawing was always a straightforward, simple, "Yes please." There was no dithering, no anxiety, and she was not frightened to try something new. She already had spirit. It was not that she was trying to show off; she was daring at the beginning because she was a novice, and she titillated the fashion press because she loved experimenting, just for the fun and enjoyment. So what if she was a little vain—if she hadn't been she would never have become the person we grew to love so much.

I soon developed a sense of how many different things the Princess had to be: a mother, a member of the royal family, the future Queen of England, an ambassador, an icon. She had all these roles to play, and, when asked, I as a designer was faced with the job of creating designs that would both reflect and enhance all of those roles.

I began to consider what I was doing in a wider, more historical context. The formality that distinguished everything the Princess wore was part of a pattern set in motion by the Queen's ancestors. It was part of a worldwide royal tradition too, and it went beyond being quintessentially English. I looked back to earlier generations, to Queen Mary and Queen Alexandra, and to their preferences for pale pastel colours and for lace and intricate detail. These luxuries suggested a more graceful, calm lifestyle and exuded a feeling of elegance.

There was of course a more modern dimension to the Princess. The press would never venture even a mildly deprecatory comment on the Queen's choice of clothing; with the young Princess nothing went unnoticed, everything was subject to the most intense scrutiny.

There were many very royal occasions that filled the calendar—Easter at Windsor, Trooping the Colour, Ascot, Balmoral, Christmas at Sandringham. The Princess was inspected in every detail on every occasion, right down to her nail varnish.

England and the world were warming to the young Princess's innate poise and charm. People wanted her to be something very special, something in their own dreams. The Princess wanted to reciprocate their love by wearing the right designs. The look had to suit the occasion and always needed to suggest that the Princess had made a real effort to look appropriate for the occasion. That did not always mean being "fashionable" if that would make people feel ill at ease. The overseas tours had not yet started and her appointments at this time were within the U.K. For Scotland it was tartan, for the country, if it were, say, a visit to a hospice, we would design a more friendly or colourful and informal suit. For London it would be something sharper for the day, and for the evening there was the demanding task of designing something that was not extravagant like you would do for a catwalk show, but something that matched her multifaceted stature as a beautiful princess, young mother, and future Queen. I had a sort of private brief to design a dignified showstopper. It was almost a contradiction.

When the foreign tours started the criteria were completely different. We had to take into consideration a variety of factors in the work schedule: the formality of state banquets, the informality of visits to remote outposts, the observation of national colours, and indigenous traditions such as picnics sitting cross-legged on the floor of a desert tent. We sometimes received notes from government departments or the British Embassy of the country to be visited giving us guidance. I recall a wonderful note which I believe originated from the British Embassy in Brasilia after the Brazilian football team had lost to Argentina in the 1990 World Cup. It was suggested that we avoid the blue, green, and yellow colours of the national team since this would seem "rather gauche," but more important, avoid the blue and white of Argentina since this could "cause a riot." There were other such communications: helicopter flights in Kathmandu where the climate had a marked diurnal variation, the necessity for sleeves to deter the mosquitos in New Delhi, and the meaning of the Korean *Taegkki* (flag). And always there had to be the formality that set the Princess apart from the crowd and showed her respect for the country in question such as little national emblems incorporated into embroidery. I could no more design what I liked than she could wear what she liked. The design had to be right for the occasion.

In the early days my business was tiny, and there was a modest cash flow, but I still bought in lengths of every colour of every fabric that I showed the Princess—not just little swatches—because I wanted to be sure that whatever I showed her would be in my hands if she chose it. If I was buying from an Italian or French mill the stock position could change daily. On top of that I held double what each garment would have needed for safety's sake. I have known a cup of tea to fall on a piece of finished work and I didn't want to let her down. Each sketch I presented meant a sizable investment. Since I had taught myself how to design and cut patterns

I hardly knew how to draw, because performing both roles meant I never needed to tell anyone else about the design until it was sewn. I used to spend hours worrying about whether the line I drew was exactly as I would cut the seam.

In a sense we were both novices at what we were doing, both developing. We were two people who had been jerked into a world to which we were not accustomed. Later, by trying hard—perhaps too hard—and exceeding everyone's expectations, we eventually became outsiders which I think increased our kinship. I didn't pretend to have all the answers, and we began to develop a way of working together that allowed us both to feel our way through the uncharted territory.

During the very early days, after the initial order of maternity dresses which was organised through *Vogue*, it fell on Anne Beckwith-Smith to help as formal drawings were passed to and fro between the Princess and me, attached with notes scribbled about colours, fabrics, and shapes. But in addition to these commissions that came directly from the Princess, some of my work continued to pass through intermediaries. It was all very hush-hush and sometimes confusing. I would be asked to design something for a "special person" and told it was for a photograph. Of course it became obvious when the photograph came out in a newspaper or magazine, but I was not told it was for the Princess. In contrast, a few years later, when our working relationship had reached a point of shorthand, I would send Diana half-finished sketches or bits of embroidery and half-made toiles for the sheer fun of exchanging ideas.

In the early days she used to come to the

shop every few weeks. Once I knew she was on her way, someone would keep vigil on the forecourt and we would close the showroom so she could look at everything without people staring at her. Then she would come to the little room upstairs to try everything on. The fever that surrounded the Princess was so intense that it attracted the good and the bad, and I know she was relieved that I never said anything about our relationship. I never explained to her why I shunned the enormous commercial capital that I could have made from her patronage, but she knew it had something to do with my unlimited thirst for technical knowledge and the sheer pleasure of the work. I think she thought I was actually incapable of exploiting her patronage. When Diana attended a film premiere in a white lace dress I had designed for her, I was puzzled to see Anne Diamond reveal on her programme the next day that I had made it. I told Diana I had no idea where the information had been leaked. Diana said, "*I* told her, and I told her to make sure she said it was a Catherine Walker dress."

There were no working meetings or fittings during her pregnancy, which accounts for why the first ten dresses I made for her were too small and all had to be remade. But later, when the clothes became more slim and skimmed the body, she would come to the showroom every few weeks. Fittings became a time of privacy and precision to which I would go armed with all the questions I needed to ask. After a year or so the relationship developed, and I used to go to her home with drawings, collection pieces, and things to be fitted. Only after my illness with cancer fifteen years later did I allow anyone else to fit Diana. In all the sixteen years I dressed

Diana, I only ever measured her three times; I actually did everything by instinct.

Often Diana became tremendously excited at the fittings and would call her dresser or the children if they were there. She was always punctual, I was never kept waiting, and in sixteen years she only cancelled two appointments. She was the easiest and most trusting of clients, and we had tremendous fun. Sometimes she would sit on the carpet correcting drawings, and I remember her delight if she loved something—she would make a noise a little like you make if you are enjoying chocolate!

Over time, the "Yes please," became "It's different," and later on, when her understanding of clothes became more European, "It's smart." Later still, when she started dressing more sexily, it was, "Eat your heart out, Brazil."

During the first few years I began to know and understand her silhouette. It was the time that I had discovered John French, and I was experimenting with the elongation of the torso. I found that the years I had spent alone as a pattern cutter and the long nights unable to sleep, working late while I dealt with the grief of widowhood, had been invaluable. My discovery of John French, his relevance to my handwriting, and my tailor George's skill all coincided at this time to fit the moment and fit Diana. I was applying my growing knowledge of men's tailoring techniques as I cut her dress patterns, and in so doing I tried to hone a clean silhouette that matched my own brief for the formality and presence I wanted Diana to have. She too saw how the slim elongation of the torso increased her poise and matched her clean smile and openness of face. But, most important during these years, as two extremely shy people in what had started out a shy relationship, we were becoming used to each other's shyness and getting to know each other more deeply.

At this time I set about creating a *fluid* silhouette. I was trying to catch the light in the camera. It was the way I felt a princess should look, but gradually she became more herself and could be herself in a way that looked naturally good in photographs. She learned what worked on camera, what would *sparkle*. I have always seen catching the light as intrinsic to my work; light and life are so close together.

I wanted my work to develop slowly because designing for someone is a very emotional thing, and I always need to start slowly for something to get into my blood. Once absorbed I can think about it in a much more unconscious way, and every six months, at the beginning of a collection, I would think about my work, and then think of Diana in the context of what I wanted to do.

I carried on designing sections of my collection each season that I knew she *wouldn't* wear. I had to do other things both because I could have become swamped by Diana and in order to move away so that I could go back and design new things for her. Also, our taste, naturally, did not always overlap. I liked the fact that she was full of surprises, unpredictable, and sometimes went for glitzy stuff that really wasn't me. I surprised her, too, and always felt that one of the good things she did was pull me back from becoming *too* poetic.

In the early eighties Diana's designs had to be more elaborate, had to look special in a particular way, and all the little details—the buttons, the binding—helped to reflect this. It felt as though Diana needed a sort of royal uniform that was a legacy from eighteenth-century English court dressing, where etiquette decreed that sartorial finery and rich apparel were appropriate. Her designs could not be simple. Later on this changed, and I worked on a look that was more pared down and less elaborate, and one that was beautiful from all angles. It was at this time I realised that focussing on the silhouette meant that designing was as much to do with the space *outside* the design as it was to do with the design itself. Often I would put different designs on a dummy and view them through a full-length mirror so that I could see every angle. I recall in particular the burgundy velvet tailcoat that we worked on for *Steel Magnolias* in 1990 which was embroidered to catch the light from the front, side, and back.

The press became her mirror. But thankfully, she was stubborn and took note of criticism by seeing for herself how she looked in the designs, not how the critics saw her. That was one of her greatest strengths: she relied on her instincts, not on me or anybody else for that matter. She worked things out for herself and she stuck to her guns.

By the mid-eighties we arrived at a point where my relationship with her became one of *total care*. Diana's first trip on her own was in 1986 to Vienna, and although I was aware of the planning, it was only when she returned, saying sweetly, "I wore all your designs" that I realised the trust she had put in me. The red and navy coatdress had indeed suited the formal day occasion perfectly, as had the white coat dress with a black waterfall detail the next day. On her last evening she wore an emerald green column sequin dress which was deliciously feminine yet formal enough for a royal princess. I was flattered by the trust as well as alerted to the enormity of the task of designing for her.

During the next few years there were up to twenty overseas tours. I think it was the tours and the trust she put in me to achieve exactly what she needed that contributed to this new and enduring phase of our relationship. I started letting her know where I was, leaving telephone numbers even if I was on holiday, making sure extra staff were always present in case of emergency.

There were times when I knew she would be wearing something I had designed for a specific occasion, and times when I was as sure as I could be that she would, only to be disappointed. I remember one such occasion on her French tour in the November of 1988. I had warned her "Don't wear any cheap clothes, the French will knock you." By that I did not mean that she should only wear my designs, but she had developed complete trust in me, and, being French, I felt I had the right to say it. We had to focus a little harder for the French tour, and when Diana saw how good the response was, she realised that these more "serious" designs had worked for her.

Diana had told me she was going to wear the Riechers lace coatdress that I had designed for her meeting with François Mitterand at the Elysée Palace. I switched on the news to watch . . . stupid mistake! Instead I saw the wonderful dress Victor Edelstein had made with the most beautiful embroidery. I wasn't so much jealous as I was energised because it was so beautiful, and it made me think that it was time for me

to look more seriously at embroidery, which until this time I had hardly touched. I didn't sleep that night. The following morning, Fay, Diana's dresser, rang with a sweet message from Diana to say that she loved all my designs and was going to start wearing them. She did indeed wear all my designs during the remainder of the visit.

My usual reaction to any setback is to work harder, and so I set to work immediately. By March 1989 my first embroidered dress was ready. Diana had asked me to do something special for her visit to the Gulf States. Before that time the embroideries I had admired in Paris were, well, French. I found them perhaps a little too heavy for Diana. I wanted something that would capture the image of an Arthurian Princess and I used the English garden as my inspiration. I also wanted a base colour that would suit the romance of the desert. It was my first piece of embroidery, and Diana had no idea what it was going to be like but was so overwhelmed when she saw it that she sent me some beautiful heart-shaped cufflinks to thank me.

By 1990 I had started designing in advance of being asked, not only because by then I was so aware and "tuned in" to her needs, but also because I was frightened by the responsibility I felt when seeing sometimes only my designs worn on foreign tours, and I wanted to be prepared.

Foreign tours were of course my most exciting commissions, but the privilege and responsibility were so potent that I tried not to think too hard about it. I was always aware how few opportunities there were or ever would be for this kind of work. On tours I could really highlight and bring to life

Diana's part in a long tradition—a world tradition—and dress her in a way that would pay her the compliment of making her stand out internationally. Of course there were some disasters and occasions when things went wrong, but my aim was always that she would come back home feeling good about herself. That was real satisfaction for me.

The disasters of course stick in my mind. On her first foreign tour to Australia in March 1983, Diana ran out of clothes. A panic telephone call came through asking for five new outfits. There was a scanty brief and a time scale of only four days. Helen, who was our principal machinist at the time, literally moved into the workroom over the Easter weekend and slept on a sofa bed. She worked on the machine as I worked at the drawing board. We started seeing the five new outfits on television from New Zealand the following Tuesday.

There was a fiasco with a long pink panné velvet evening dress which Diana wore in Palm Beach, Florida, on her first trip to the United States back in 1985. I did not always have the time to test the ideas technically that I suggested to Diana. It was elaborately draped, and the cowl neck and the fabric fought each other. It was my first experience with cutting panné this way and the more I looked at it the more I could only see agitation. It looked wonderful in the newspapers but all I could see was agitation.

On another occasion George rang me and said "I've got a problem." It emerged that while he was pressing a richly embroidered full-length white lace coat dress that I had designed for Diana's State Banquet at Château de Chambord in France in November 1988, he had left a scorch mark on the inner lining. I rang Diana's dresser in a panic, and she decided not to mention it. I finally confessed years later, and needless to say, Diana giggled about it.

The challenges of the kind of work demanded for the different tours were endless. They often meant weeks of solitary research and work. Each time Diana went on tour it reminded me of the days at school when I took exams. Would I pass? Had I done enough homework? The research was often an education in itself. I was learning all sorts of odd things about Japanese colours for mourning, Czech folk costume, Indian marquetry, Indonesian flowers, Nigerian batik prints, and even what braids represented which rank in foreign military uniform.

Perhaps the most effort went into a dress for Rome. In 1985 Diana asked me to design something for her historic meeting with the Pope. I went to Rome to the Vatican and interviewed some officials for guidance on protocol, but curiously there were no guidelines apart from the obvious restrictions on being covered up. I spent hours at the Vatican library looking for precedents. The best I could find was Sophia Loren. In a cafe facing St. Peter's Square I was chatting to a nun who told me that Catholic queens were the only ones who didn't have to wear black. Apart from that I could do whatever I wanted. I was aware that such an occasion was not one for making a "fashion statement." I had gone to Rome to try and absorb the surroundings, and I felt that a dress rather than a suit would fit the occasion and be softer, more humble. I hoped the international press would understand this and would judge Diana in terms of the occasion for which it was needed. We had to be completely generous in the face of criticism and do homage to the occasion. In the event she was applauded.

Luckily, I loved doing these very specific things and was driven by the challenge and the desire to get everything absolutely right for her. The fashion world takes itself so seriously, but I saw Diana as above all that. My designs had to work for her job, which was not always glamorous. The reality was she could be meeting officials as well as lepers or AIDS patients, and the right designs were part of the nitty-gritty of the job.

Diana was also an intuitive dresser; she did not primarily dress for the fashion intelligentsia. As the most photographed woman in history, she was dressing for a very wide audience, and in doing so she touched many hearts.

Together we would look at the press reaction and how she came across in print—for her an emotional reaction but for me a technical one. Designing for a catwalk show or designing for clients in the showroom was far different from designing for someone whose image was minutely scrutinised in flat print or flat screen. It took me years to realise that my sleeve heads (shoulders) were a quarter of an inch too wide for her because of the proportion of head to shoulder on screen. She would look great when she put one on, but it didn't work on screen or in photographs.

It was easier to design for some countries than for others. India and Indonesia were like invitations to dream. Hong Kong and Thailand were exotic because she could wear all the strong colours. The UAE was a blaze of flame bedouin dye-colours: for Egypt I felt she needed earth colours and for Pakistan I chose green with beaten gold.

Saudi Arabia was immensely romantic but had to be proper; Australia was young and spirited; Brazil shimmered; and America had to top the "seen-that-done-that" audience.

As we became more attuned, the warning periods got shorter, and I'd typically get a "By the way, next month I'm going to Hungary," and we'd have to work out what engagements she would have over that period and judge the pace and balance of the wardrobe. Sometimes it was a fax to say she was off in three weeks. All through the years my response would always be one of both absolute delight and panic.

If I had to pick the most exciting commission I was asked to design for any tour, it would have to be the design for the enthronement of Emperor Akihito. The whole world was impressed by how this girl had developed into the epitome of a Princess. She shone in the ice-blue sheath that brought out the deep blue of her eyes behind the veil. The full-length coatdress was modern yet suitably formal for the importance of the enthronement, and when I watched her I truly felt her stature set her apart in every meaning of the word. It was thrilling for me.

One day in 1986 Diana came into my office wearing a Chris Clyne shirt dress, and I told her how good she looked and meant it. I think that was the point at which she realised that I just wanted her to look good no matter whose clothes she was wearing. I also think it was difficult for her to appreciate it when someone saw the real person in her and not just the image. It was the start of another part of the *total care* which has remained secret, but which I do not think Diana would have minded me talking about now. After about five years there was a clear understanding of what worked for Diana, and if she felt like a colour or theme that she knew was not me, she could still apply the same criteria and find it at another designer. She would come in regularly with other designers' things and say "Could you make this work please?" It wasn't just resetting a sleeve or lengthening the waist. I am sure that on more than one occasion the original designer must have looked at the newspapers and thought, "Isn't that rather like something I did?" I felt it my duty to offer her a complete service and could not have turned those requests down. They were not trivial requests; she had a job to do and trusted me to take some of the pressure of that job in the same way one might turn to an elder sister for help.

Along with the designs for tours, there was of course the private side of Diana that needed to reflect, like landmarks, the changing circumstances she faced. We all dress to some extent according to our needs: shorter lengths to feel more sexy, red to show we are not upset, curvaceous clothes to send messages to other women to back off, pinstripe to be one of the boys, significant clothes for lunches with fashion editors. Clothes were even more a form of language for Diana, because she had spent all of her adult life dressed up for a royal job. The last state dress I made for Diana was for a private reception at Buckingham Palace in November 1992, just after her separation. She wanted to look old-fashioned and traditional. It was a classic 1950s-cut evening dress, and we chose formal full-skirted silk duchesse satin in buttermilk, with traditional pearl and sequin embroidery.

There were lonely times for her. People wanted to love Diana, the press wanted her image over and over again, *Vogue* had her on its cover, intellectuals wanted to analyse her, and of course we designers dreamed of dressing her. The contrast between this wonderfully desirable image and the reality of her private unhappiness was too much for her to live with, and her grief became my sadness.

It was very hard for her after the separation. She had lost some of the love in her heart in her struggle to survive and her clothes became demure for a period for two reasons. First, she was vulnerable and upset and could only make a statement of how she felt through what she wore, and second, I suspect, out of respect for her children.

This was certainly one of the stages when Diana could have stopped coming to me, and the press, who always anticipated a change of style every time she changed her hair, was suggesting that she would go to other designers for a new look. Over the years several newcomers were hailed as the new designer in Diana's life. I can't pretend it wasn't hurtful when a headline ran, "Who is going to dress the Princess now that she is separated?" and when a Sunday newspaper suggested Diana should wear the clothes of a designer who I genuinely did not believe was able to do the job. However, if she was going to go in a direction that was outside my handwriting, I would have been the one to leave and not try to compete.

I felt aware of these various suggestions but not insecure. After all, she didn't belong to me. What I found hurtful was that the suggestions sometimes seemed to be made for political reasons and not to help Diana. I wanted to make sure she stayed with me because I loved her, and I worked even harder because indirectly she always made me aware that I needed to change too. Every time I'm under pressure I go back to work.

It is a myth that Diana, apart from at a very early stage, wore only British designers out of patriotic duty and a myth that it was too much trouble for her to find new designers. Diana took her work very seriously indeed. She was ruthless when it came to the look that went with the job, and if the designer who could deliver it lived in the South Pole she would have gone there. There was no obligation to any one designer, just expedience, and I never expected anything less. We both knew that our professional and personal relationships were separate entities.

In February 1993, following the separation, Diana came to look at my new collection. I was surprised, but so was she: "I thought I'd only order a couple of things," she said. She ordered six or seven, the same amount she usually ordered at the start of each season. I had completely rethought, and the collection had become stronger. The designs were more relaxed and younger. I couldn't have done it before, but it was what I wanted to do now. The demure phase was over and so was her marriage, but what I hadn't anticipated was how quickly she would change and begin wearing more of both my casual wear and my sexier evening wear. Her trip to Versailles was one of those moments. She wore the black dress long before I expected her to. It was very *décolleté*—more suited to Los Angeles than to the formality of Paris. Her purpose was to shock and to reassert herself as a beautiful woman. It made another, subtler statement—she was still a Princess, and she was untouchable.

By this time her looks and physique had changed dramatically since she had first come to see me as a pale, slightly plump but fragile-looking girl. Now she was tanned, fitter, more muscular. She had become a perfectionist, working very hard on her body because of the scrutiny it was under and to help keep her sane through her marital upheaval. She was not a neat, compact, polished little doll; she was tall and rangy, narrow-hipped, with muscles, a bust, and strong legs. I was dressing a *real* body, full of corners, and the designs had to enhance this new beauty, not just hang from the shoulders. This was not an invitation to design light, fragile clothes or broken images.

Up to this point Diana was ordering mostly commission pieces from me, but things were changing, and she had begun to order clothes that had not been designed specifically for her—the Versailles dress was one such. She was also wearing more international designers in public. I was happy both for her *and* for myself, for if you dress someone you want them to look good all the time. There was a new radiance about her, and when I look back at my working notes of the time, I am reminded that we had talked about trying to capture that: how the designs should *smile*. Little by little I had seen her silhouette and her colouring change and I was more enthralled than ever by the designs that brought out this new image.

And then in the spring of 1995, when I was really revelling in my new designing, I found I had breast cancer. I had to let go, and it was not easy emotionally. I didn't want to, but I was in what I can only describe as a kind of twister when I was ill. Anyone can guess that dressing Diana was often a cause for jealousy and bitchiness. Meaning so much to so many, Diana provoked the best and worst in people, and dressing her, I often did too. But I never told her because she was coping with enormous pressure already.

I had to accept the possibility that that was it; that I could no longer provide Diana with the *total care* that I had until then. I had always played the strong role with her and had never been the vulnerable one. For the time being I needed the space to look at my own life. I pulled back, we stopped exchanging professional ideas as frequently as we had, and I stopped doing all the fittings.

In September 1996, after the treatment and a period of recuperation, I had made up my mind. Because I could no longer provide Diana with the total commitment she had had from me, I decided to call it a day. I went to see her to tell her that I couldn't go on, but when I met her I knew I couldn't stop. Diana, by developing her international status as a charity worker and a beautiful woman, was regaining her self-esteem, mending her heart. She was more at peace with herself. It was wonderful to see and I wanted to be part of that new growth, that new future. Slowly we started working together again but in a different way, at a pace that suited me. And having been freed up, I in turn was able to change direction again.

My work had become younger before the cancer, and after, it became younger still. I enjoyed our last year together tremendously. My illness had turned everything around: I could do things that were a little bit madder, a bit more sexy, and it was exciting because I had more time. My work was lighter, younger, more fun, and happier. I was designing better because I was more relaxed.

Similarly, Diana could afford to dispense with the royal image to some extent, and what I call the "rock image" had superseded it. It was somehow fitting that she was more the star now.

Perhaps because I was always trying to do something that helped her to move on, she always came back. I wanted to go on providing all the answers I could. My dream from the beginning had been to deal with Diana as a *real person*—to me it was as important as the designing. I was aware from an early date that, in a way, Diana did not exist in people's minds as a real person but as an image. I often thought that it was one of the most unfair parts of her life. It's not possible for anyone to live, to survive, in that position.

Designing for the real person meant I had constantly to focus. It was not easy to strip away the public image and discard it totally, it was something I worked at. More than once she said to me "I don't like being used." She would always be surrounded by opportunistic people, not just designers, but I was determined not to use her. This wasn't difficult, for the commercial gain was unimportant to me, and although the fashion politics did hurt me, I did not understand them enough to interact with them.

When I was first approached about the auction of Diana's dresses at the end of 1996, my initial reaction was that I wanted to buy all my dresses back. Naively I had not understood what a major event lay ahead, I just didn't want them to be scattered around the globe. In a funny way, while they were all still where she kept them at Kensington Palace, I felt I was still in touch with them. On top of that, once I realised how prominent I would be, and quite how many of my designs were involved, there was also the embarrassing aspect of seeing just how much some of then had become dated. However, when it became clear that both charities involved, AIDS and cancer, were likely to benefit hugely, I gave it everything I could. I watched her and Meredith Etherington-Smith set about it with the same energy and professionalism that she went on to give to her work with the land mines. She wanted me to be with her at the London party at Christie's, prior to the auction in New York. She knew what an important event it was for me, too, as it was my first public event since I had contracted cancer in 1995. I had been inundated by calls from the press, but, as usual, I spoke to no one. I found it very unsettling as I was still recovering, but as always it was ultimately, her show not mine. It was enough for me to be there that evening and support the event and Diana, who, in wanting me there with her, was showing how much I had meant to her through the years. She was shedding a part of her earlier life and preparing for a new future.

After that time we felt a return to the instinctive understanding and communication between us that we had lost during my illness. I felt I knew what she was thinking and feeling, and when she was going to ring me. My staff think I am nuts because for years I seemed to know when Diana was going to ring me and I was right so often they grudgingly had to admit it may have been more than coincidence. So she did one day in mid-August and told me she wanted to see me. I guessed it was important. I had already

June, 1997.

Diana and I share a joke at Christie's Gala Evening, London, to support the auction of her dresses to be held in New York on 25 June 1997.

Photographer: Tim Graham

been thinking about how she would have to move on, that we were finished with the swimming-costume-top evening dresses. I anticipated that she would move on to wear more mid-Atlantic clothes. I felt thrilled that Diana could at last control her own image. The real person had finally become strong enough to supersede the image. I was looking forward to this new phase with relish.

She came to see me two days later. She tried twice to come through the front entrance but could not because of a photographer. After driving around for a while and speaking to me on her mobile she eventually came in through a side door. She ordered a long knee-length jacket in dark navy with a royal blue pinstripe. She also ordered a burnt red draped cocktail dress with a cowl neck. She had tried several things including a long, white tuxedo dress which she loved. I made a mental note, knowing she'd come back for it. Later, I changed my mind about the pinstripe and thought it would look clearer in white, and about the cocktail dress which I changed to crimson.

I dropped her a note to remind her of what she had ordered and mentioned the changes. She rang to say thank you, both things were fine, and I too said thank you to her. We didn't normally thank each other this much. She was thanking me for the *total care*, and I was thanking her for the trust. I thought no more about it but that was our last conversation—five days later Diana was dead.

I still had one more commission for Diana, Princess of Wales. Paul Burrell rang requesting a dress for Diana to be buried in. It is not a dress I wish to describe or talk about; it is private between the few people who know about it. I know that had she lived, it is one she would most probably have bought and loved. While it was undoubtedly the saddest and most difficult commission of my life, just being asked to do it made me feel relieved and immensely grateful. Paul's reaction to my dress was, "She will be covered in love." I am still a part of her life forever in a way, and a little part of me will be with her forever.

November 1997

Kensington Palace, May 1997.

Diana, Princess of Wales, with me and some of my staff who had worked on her clothes for the auction at Christie's that benefited the AIDS and cancer charities that the Princess supported. CLOCKWISE FROM TOP LEFT: Carmel, Amrat, Audrey, Edda, Grace, Linda, Helen, Gerda, Elena, myself, Lida, Diana, Princess of Wales, Regina, and Carmelita.

In April 1997, the Princess invited me to bring the staff of my first workroom to Kensington Palace. She wanted to mark the occasion of the auction of her clothes with a private meeting with the people who had carried out the work.

My staff were of course delighted and honoured with such a personal meeting. Some of them had been making clothes for the Princess since the early months of her marriage in 1981 but had never met her. They entered the palace with trepidation and excitement. The room was almost like a meeting of the United Nations—an English Princess, myself a Frenchwoman, and staff members from Brazil, Germany, India, Italy, Jamaica, Lebanon, Persia, Portugal, Thailand, and Woolwich! The room buzzed with different accents and laughter.

The Princess laughingly held up each dress and said something like "So who made this—Paris 1988?" and the seamstress would proudly raise her hand. "And what about this—New York 1995?" In the space of a morning, sixteen years of memories were raised and discussed—royal tours, charity galas, meetings with emperors and kings, difficult fabrics, embroidery that was worked on through the night to meet a deadline, last-minute alterations that made all the difference. Carmelita, who had proudly claimed the green smock that the Princess wore to leave St. Mary's Hospital after the birth of Prince William, was unwell at first and

suffered from claustrophobia in the crowded room. The Princess was the first to notice her distress and literally ran across the room to hand her a glass of water before anyone else had noticed her discolouring face and slightly swaying stance.

Although the Princess and I had not conferred about what we should wear for the picture, she was sure I would wear a trouser suit so she did as well. She was right, and we both turned up wearing what looked like an arranged dress code. Curiously, in all those years she and I had never stood together deliberately to be photographed and there was some rivalry about who was taller. For this picture we sat down.

Before that day my staff had been full of questions. Should they curtsey? What should they say? But the morning passed in a haze of enjoyment. One small meeting demonstrated the Princess's ability to bring people together and make each person feel special in a most unique way.

A few days later each member of the staff received a framed and signed photograph as a memento from the Princess. Each parcel was carefully wrapped in navy blue paper and tied with a silk bow.

Photographer: Tim Graham

Pearls and Drapes

Sequin and oyster pearl embroidered dress and tailored bolero with Elizabethan collar.

Commissioned by HRH The Princess of Wales, November 1989.

This private commission was designed for an important official visit to Hong Kong in November 1989. The embroidery was by S. Lock Ltd., and I chose pearls because they seemed so appropriate for a visit to the Orient. Although the inspiration for the collar was Elizabethan, it led people to rename the piece the "Elvis dress"!

Whenever I saw the Princess in this dress I could not help but feel that it would not be possible for anyone else ever to wear this dress and bolero. She shone in the dress and the dress shone around her in a shimmering column of glistening pearls.

The Princess wore this dress when she was guest of honour at the British Fashion Awards at the Royal Albert Hall in London in October 1989. The Princess was aware of the irony that I was not even nominated and sent me a touching letter that read, "Dearest Catherine, To <u>my</u> best designer of the year, fondest love from Diana."

At the time there was much speculation over how many pearls had been hand embroidered onto the dress. We have no idea although some newspapers estimated 20,000. What is not apparent from the pictures is the weight of the dress, which was immense.

The dress caused great excitement in the Christie's auction, and I was delighted that so much money was raised for breast cancer and AIDS charities.

Photographer: Tim Graham

AUTUMN/WINTER COLLECTION 1994/95

Long jacket in white Buche silk velvet with grapevine embroidery in white and ivory pearls and stitchwork.

In September 1994, Harpers & Queen commissioned a jacket for a story called "White Lines." I chose white silk velvet because it is so sumptuous. The jacket is featured over a gently flared silk crepe catsuit.

Photographers: Tyen / The National Magazine Company Ltd., Stephen Hayward (detail)

SPRING/SUMMER COLLECTION 1993

Asymmetric dress with graduated pearl embroidery in oyster silk crepe drap by Hurel.

The English complexion lends itself to the cool opalescence of pearls, and I often found myself returning to their softness in various forms. Embroidery is an obvious example, and here the pearls are used to emulate the draping of fabric across the curve of the bodice.

Photographer: Stephen Hayward

Suits de Rigueur

**Navy and white Dormeuil
barathea two-tone suit**

Commissioned by HRH The Princess of Wales
for an official visit to Japan, March 1986.

*Our research for commissions often started by
discreetly quizzing other clients. I discovered through
our questioning that navy is a traditional colour in
Japan that represents formality. The contrast of the
navy and white emphasises the tall silhouette.
The sharpness of this contrast was softened by the
absence of formal lapels and revers. The Princess
arrived in Japan wearing this suit, and I was
amused to see that the prime minister's wife met
her in a matching navy and white suit.*

*Navy and white, and black and white are
also traditional Ascot colours and the suit was
subsequently worn at Ascot in June that year.*

Photographer: Tim Graham

opposite

AUTUMN/WINTER COLLECTION **1990**

**Black and white cut-away jacket in fine
Agnona Prince of Wales check.**

Harpers & Queen, October 1990:
"Beyond the Pale."

Cecil Beaton's work for My Fair Lady *was a perfect
example of black and white as an alternative to
pastel colours so customary for formal occasions in the
English summer. It is used here in a fine check wool.*

Photographer: François Halard / The National Magazine Company Ltd.

Hat by Andrew Wilkie, Joseph

"Colonial Suit" in cream Corisia washed silk with scooped neckline and pleated skirt.

Commissioned by HRH The Princess of Wales for a state visit to Indonesia in October 1989 and worn again at RAF Cranwell, July 1991.

The colours, climate, and landscape of Indonesia all combined to influence the design of this suit. The scoop-neck and three-quarter sleeves were cool, yet formal enough for the occasion, and the cream washed silk swayed in the hot breeze.

Because of its reminiscence of the Raj, the suit was suitable for a military occasion back home. The Princess covers her ears to protect herself from the noise of a Vulcan bomber during a fly-past at the end of a passing-out parade at the airbase.

Photographers: PA News (this page), R.A.F. Cranwell / REX Features (opposite)

Hat by Philip Somerville

Fuchsia pink flared frock coat in soft Moreau wool.

Commissioned by HRH The Princess of Wales in 1992 for the Garter Ceremony, Windsor, June 1993.

The late eighties and early nineties were known for the type of power dressing associated with the suit worn by Cecilia Chancellor on page 32. As the mood moved away from this, I softened my tailoring, not at the shoulder but lower, by adding a little width, as seen here, which gives a more fluid and softer silhouette.

The fuchsia colour of the Princess's outfit contrasted with the holders of the Order, who wear long black velvet robes and brightly coloured feathered hats.

The Most Noble Order of the Garter is the oldest existing monarchical order of chivalry, comprising the Sovereign, The Prince of Wales, and twenty-four Knights Companions. In addition, there are now Royal Knights, Foreign Knights, and Ladies of the Order. Her Majesty The Queen presides over the Garter Day service, held traditionally at St. George's Chapel, Windsor Castle, to install the new Knights.

Photograph by Alpha
Hat by Marina Kilerry

opposite

SPRING/SUMMER COLLECTION 1994

Open jacket and high-waisted skirt in beige Agnona herringbone wool and silk.

Tatler, October 1993: "Altar Egos."

Amanda Pays wears this herringbone suit as a wedding guest. The fluidity of the open jacket has become a part of my handwriting. The horn buttons emphasize the elongation of the midriff and add a slightly military formality to the suit.

Photographer: John Swannell / The Condé Nast Publications Ltd.

SPRING/SUMMER
COLLECTION **1995**

**Black wool edge-to-edge jacket
with fitted shift.**

"Catherine Walker goes from
strength to strength—her couture
womenswear for summer is superb."
Vogue diary, 1995.

*The lack of buttons gives this jacket a
minimalist feeling, and the black
satinized wool complements the pared-
down effect. The proportion is balanced
by the three-quarter sleeves, the low-cut
neckline, and the equal length of the
jacket and shift. The patent belt punctu-
ates the austerity of the wool.*

Photographer: David Mignon
Hat by Maison Michel, Paris,
for Catherine Walker

opposite

SPRING/SUMMER
COLLECTION **1996**

**Summer suit in almond green
Agnona wool.**

Harpers & Queen, May 1996:
"Ascot Gavotte."

*The round shoulderline and the mini-
malism of the design adds a younger feel
to a traditional Ascot suit. Suitably
modelled by Mrs. Henry Cecil, wife of
the British horse trainer, this suit
beautifully conveys the flattery of pale
colours to the English complexion.*

Photographer: Martyn Thompson
Hat by Philip Treacy

Grand coatdress in ice blue Taroni silk.

Commissioned by HRH The Princess of Wales. Enthronement ceremony of Emperor Akihito of Japan, November 1990.

The commission of a dress for HRH The Princess of Wales to wear at the enthronement of the emperor of Japan presented a great challenge. The grand coatdress style reflected the formality of the official visit while also allowing an element of youthfulness, fluidity, and graceful movement. The very pale blue colour was chosen as a traditional colour of Japanese state occasions and the embroidered Prince of Wales feathers were representative of the United Kingdom. The embroidery was curved gently towards the waist and over the hips in order to contrast with the sharpness of the tailoring. The plastron effect across the chest gives a touch of military formality.

While custom and protocol dictated many design decisions, I was always aware that the Princess looked stunning in ice blue as it so flattered her peaches-and-cream complexion and brought out the full depth of her blue eyes.

Photograph by Photographers International

Veiled headband by Philip Somerville

opposite

SPRING/SUMMER COLLECTION **1995**

Powder blue belted suit in satinized Garigue wool.

Vogue, March 1995: "The Strong Suit."

Summer 1995 saw a return to more womanly dressing with the clinched waist and more defined shoulders. In this picture, Yasmin Ghauri wears this 1940s-style icy blue suit that plays against the background of the new Eurostar station.

Photographer: Neil Kirk / The Condé Nast Publications Ltd.

**Portrait of Linda Evange-
lista in a waltzing dress in
Redaelli silk velvet with
embroidered silk roses,
cording, and jets.**

*Liz Tilberis chose this dress
for an international couture
feature in the October 1991
issue of* Vogue.

Photographers: Patrick Demarchelier /
The Condé Nast Publications Ltd.,
Stephen Hayward (detail)

Victorian Influences

AUTUMN/WINTER
COLLECTION 1990/91

**Grand fringed dress in black Buche
silk velvet.**

*The knotted passementerie effect—traditionally
found with fringing—has been replaced by
embroidery that echoes the effect. The embroidery around the hip, cuff, and collar of the
dress is also used to illuminate the density of
the velvet. The fringing provides a fluid movement to the dress.*

Photographer: Yoshie Nishikawa

opposite

AUTUMN/WINTER
COLLECTION 1990/91

**Blackwatch silk tartan dress and wrap
with asymmetric Hurel hand fringing.**

*The proportions of a traditional Victorian dress
are altered by the displacement of the waist
and the circular positioning of the fringing.
The illusion is one of elongation while
maintaining the charm of the original form.*

Photographer: Platon

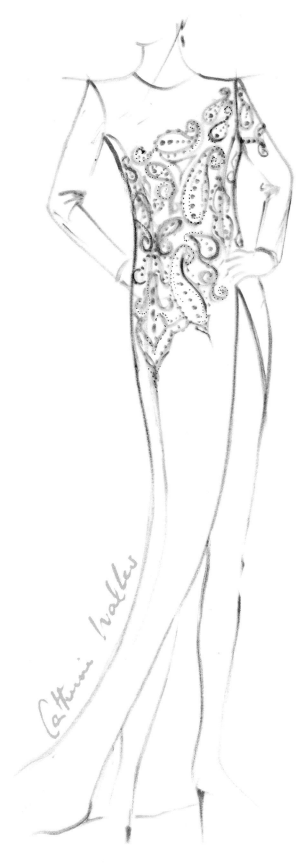

AUTUMN/WINTER COLLECTION 1991/92

Deep green Bouton Renaud velvet dress with black jet paisley embroidery.

The pattern of the embroidery was inspired by a Victorian scarf, and the positioning imitates the way a shawl is draped over the body and falls to the hip which is then emphasized by a high split.

Much of the Autumn/Winter 1991/92 collection was inspired by this same Victorian scarf.

Photographer: Yoshie Nishikawa

AUTUMN/WINTER
COLLECTION 1990/91

**Hand-beaded fringed
halterneck dress.**

*The fringed beading takes the vertical
line of the tartan as a graphic. The
effect is a new colour scheme that
echoes the original Blackwatch tartan
but in catching the light adds a
luminescence of its own. The modern
halterneck shape contrasts with
the richness of the hand-fringed
embroidery.*

Photographer: Stephen Hayward
Photographed with the kind
permission of Perdita Hay

Midnight blue silk faille one-shouldered ballgown with soft princess-line skirt and paisley embroidery over loose fringing.

The jet beading is inspired by the design of Indian Pashmina shawls and depicts the most common motif used—the Pine, later known as the Paisley pattern.

Photographer: Stephen Hayward

Diamanté and Filigree

Black draped silk crepe dress with diamante bodice.

Commissioned by HRH The Princess of Wales to attend a banquet hosted by Vice President Dr. Shanka Dayal Sharma at the former palace of the Nizam of Hyderabad, India, February 1992.

This dress was commissioned for an official visit to India. The more research I did for this dress the more I became lost in the rich complex pattern of Indian culture and its hybridisation with the British influence of the Raj. I knew the Princess was intending to wear the Spencer tiara, and my daughter Marianne found a beautiful book for me on the decorative art of India, in which I came upon a sandalwood and ivory inlaid casket whose design seemed to complement the tiara perfectly. The technical design of the embroidery drew upon this traditional pattern of marquetry, and the flatness of the stones is also particular to Indian jewellery.

Photographers: Dave Chancellor / Alpha, Stephen Hayward (detail)

Marriage of Lady Helen Windsor and Mr. Timothy Taylor, St. George's Chapel, Windsor Castle, 18 July 1992.

The design of a wedding dress is the ultimate gift a designer can give to a client. When Lady Helen Windsor asked me to make her wedding dress in January 1992 I was thrilled and excited but also conscious of the immense responsibility that I had undertaken. The dress would of course come under scrutiny by the fashion press, but I was aware that it could only be judged a real success if Helen felt that this was the dress of her dreams.

The initial preparations included taking the bride through a multitude of design variations, gradually honing in on the style we thought was right: a gently flared panel dress in silk zibeline with a pearl and diamond embroidered curled neckline and cathedral-length train.

The planning stages were rigorously thorough. We visited St. George's chapel in order to gauge the correct length of the train, studied the Kent tiara Helen would wear, and sampled embroidery variations in order to find the most beautiful. Details such as the Gothic curves of the chapel windows and the pattern of diamonds in the tiara were then incorporated into the design.

The dress was cut in ten panels: each one was full length in order to emphasize the fluidity of the body. It was not the easiest of constructions. One tiny mistake in the neckline and the whole dress would have been rendered unusable. My team, headed by Aila, the pattern cutter, realized this and, although technically they are the best in the business, they were apprehensive of working on the dress. At times I almost had to bribe them to work on it. We resorted to shutting Edda, the sample machinist, in a room on her own as she slowly worked away. It was one of the longest processes I had ever undertaken in my work.

Several weeks before her wedding date Lady Helen tried the dress on for her mother, HRH The Duchess of Kent. She looked every inch the radiant and beautiful bride and was touchingly pleased

with the dress. But I had a nagging doubt in my mind. Throughout her engagement Helen had unconsciously lost weight. Her figure was now very slight and the dress, although allowing for this measurement alteration, seemed to me to be slightly out of proportion. Although imperceptible to a casual observer, the shoulderline did not appear to be "anchored" correctly for the overall harmony of the line.

I agonized over the problem all weekend. I genuinely thought I had made a mistake on one of the most important dresses I would ever create. I knew the only solution was to re-cut the original shoulderline and alter the construction in order to emphasize the waistline.

On Monday morning I hesitantly approached my staff and explained the situation. They did not even query my request and with utter professionalism commenced work again. The final dress was exactly right. The bride never knew of the intervening saga. When Lady Helen Windsor walked down the aisle I knew I had given her my best.

(*below*) Photographer: Christopher Simon-Sykes / Camera Press (*opposite*) Photograph courtesy of Lady Helen Taylor

opposite

SPRING/SUMMER COLLECTION 1994

Tiara jacket in navy Clerici shantung silk over white-washed silk palazzo jumpsuit.

HRH The Duchess Of Kent, July 1994.

HRH The Duchess of Kent has long been a supporter of my work and was a great comfort to me during my illness. She is probably one of the most generous people I know.

This season's collection had many ethnic influences, one of which was a beautiful nineteenth-century Hungarian man's vest with richly ornate handwork around the arm scye and neck opening. In a crossover of ethnic mixtures I merged this in a diamante and pearl embroidery border inspired by Queen Mary's "festoon-and-scroll" tiara made by Garrard in 1893.

HRH The Duchess of Kent kindly agreed to an interview with Tamasin Day-Lewis. When asked about the Princess she commented:

"Catherine said she wouldn't take the two of us. I wanted to go there passionately and kept on at her, and eventually she said she could dress me—a bit! After that, I was always allowed in to see a collection, but second. Whenever I saw something on the rail I really wanted, it had always gone to Diana.

"The thing about Catherine is that her judgment is always right. She has stopped me from having things I wanted. I remember something in satin and wool stripes, and she said no to the colour. This gentle, rather timid person has an inner strength that I could only imagine. We don't see her showing it except when she thinks she's right and you think you are, and you are swayed by her conviction. It is an infinitely compelling combination. In her designs she is so strong.

"What I feel is that it is an absolute privilege to wear her clothes. You feel you can't let her down. On one occasion, I asked her to make something for a state visit. I had an aquamarine tiara, but no necklace. Catherine suggested copying the pattern of the tiara onto the neck and bodice in embroidery and blue stones. I was resistant initially, but the result was beautiful; tiny and delicate with minute stones, and it didn't look overdone. It was so subtle. The dress was pale blue, and she had used the aquamarine and pearl of the tiara. I went to such lengths to get the details right. I couldn't let the dress down. You have to keep her standards."

Photographer: Patrick Demarchelier

below

Shalwar kameez in aquamarine Taroni georgette with tiara embroidery.

Wedding of Jemima Goldsmith and Imran Khan, 21 June 1995.

This was a rare private commission when I was undergoing radiotherapy, and it boosted my system to dress such a lovely bride. Diana, Princess of Wales, had recommended us to her friend Jemima. We had previously made one of these traditional outfits for the Princess for a working visit to Pakistan.

The tiara embroidery represented a European influence to contrast with the traditional dress of Pakistan.

Photograph by REX Features

AUTUMN/WINTER COLLECTION 1993/94

The following "diamanté" collection has its origins in Cartier's "Garland Style" jewellery which could have been worn with sinuous gowns by Frederick Worth in mauve, straw, hydrangea blue, or maize. However, Cartier used to borrow black velvet from Worth to display his jewellery and it seemed most appropriate to me for this embroidery. The soot-black silk velvet is the perfect base for the icy clear diamanté and silver filigree work.

All photography: Stephen Hayward

left

Tiara dress in black Buche silk velvet.

The design of a tiara has been used as edging to both the neck and cap sleeves of the dress in order to frame the neck and arms.

center

Bow dress in black Buche silk velvet

This dress was inspired by a diamond ribbon bow pendant brooch in circular hand drop-shaped diamonds. The ribbons of the bow have been absorbed into the narrow straps of the dress.

right

T-Bar choker dress in black Buche silk velvet.

This dress was inspired by the shape of the draperie de decolleté *necklaces and the geometric shapes of bandeaux tiaras. The vertical positioning of the bandeau from the nape of the neck and down the back emphasizes the sensuality of the spine.*

CHOKER DRESS IN BLACK
BUCHE SILK VELVET.
*The form of Cartier Resille (hairnet)
jewellery is used for a stomacher
effect to create the shape of an
Edwardian choker embroidered in
diamanté and filigree work.*

Tuxedo Moods

AUTUMN/WINTER COLLECTION 1990/91

Short bib-jacket in black Bouton Renaud silk velvet with white chalk beads.

The pattern of the chalk beads emulates the Venetian gros point of the bib-fronted bands of raised lace in the late seventeenth century and was typical in France during the period of the Trois Mousquetaires.

Photographer: Yoshie Nishikawa

opposite left

AUTUMN/WINTER COLLECTION 1992/93

Black barathea Agnona tuxedo with white Moreau ottoman collar, lapels, and turned-back cuffs, and waistcoat with black jet buttons.

HRH The Princess of Wales, as patron of the Benesh Institute and the Huntington's Disease Association, attends a gala performance of *Design for Dance* at Her Majesty's Theatre in Haymarket, November 1993.

This waistcoat under a sleek-fitting tuxedo is my approach to "layering" which strongly influenced this season. Layering, by its very nature, is generally a soft outlined, loose-fitting effect and could not be farther from my handwriting, which has always been body-skimming and structured.

This suit was designed with men's trousers for the 1992 winter collection but the Princess asked for me to make it with a short skirt. It was her first public engagement after the announcement of her separation.

Photograph by REX Features

opposite right

Black V-front tuxedo with cuff-link buttons and strapless white dress in Agnona wool.

HRH The Princess of Wales at the Symphony for the Spire concert, Salisbury Cathedral, September 1992.

The Princess was accompanied by HRH The Prince of Wales for a visit to Salisbury cathedral for a Royal Gala Concert, a fund-raising event to restore the spire, tower, and west front of the cathedral. This jacket was originally worn as part of a short tuxedo pants suit, but the Princess asked me to suggest a replacement for the trousers for a late summer evening. We agreed on the design of this V-front strapless white wool dress to complement the jacket.

Photographer: Tim Graham

AUTUMN/WINTER COLLECTION 1995/96

**Black Dormeuil wool barathea and double satin tuxedo
with trompe l'oeil camisole effect.**

*This trompe l'oeil effect would have been found on a 1930s spring
day suit, perhaps with a white piqué bib on a light tweed. Here, it is
translated into a sharp masculine tuxedo, which is softened by the
femininity of a cleavage bustier dress with vest effect.*

Photographer: Yoshie Nishikawa

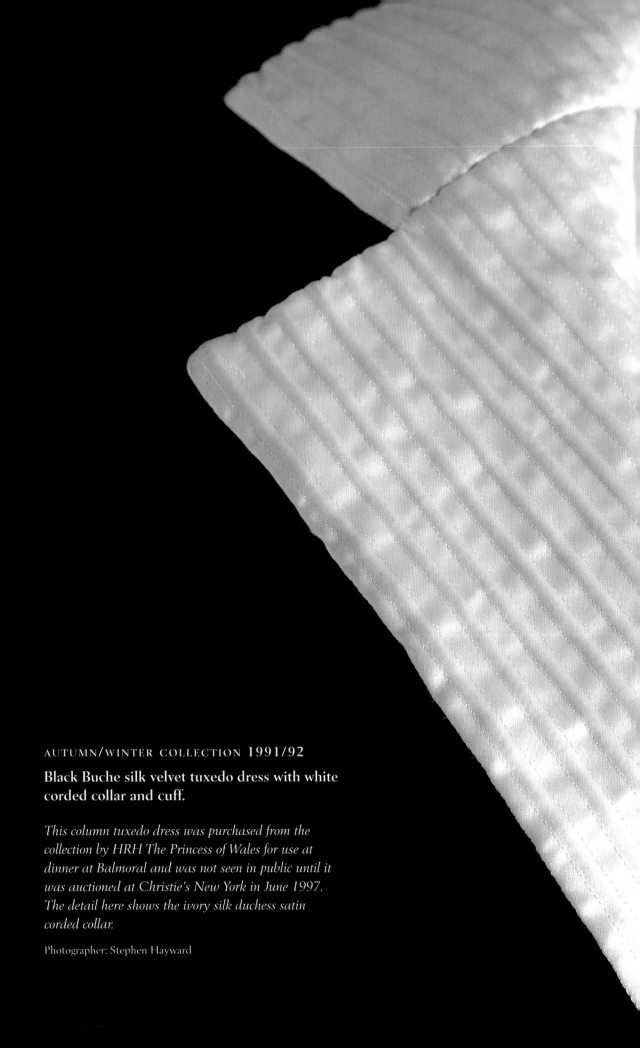

AUTUMN/WINTER COLLECTION 1991/92

Black Buche silk velvet tuxedo dress with white corded collar and cuff.

This column tuxedo dress was purchased from the collection by HRH The Princess of Wales for use at dinner at Balmoral and was not seen in public until it was auctioned at Christie's New York in June 1997. The detail here shows the ivory silk duchess satin corded collar.

Photographer: Stephen Hayward

AUTUMN/WINTER COLLECTION 1996/97

Grand tuxedo double-breasted evening dress in Clerici silk drap with short V-train. Taroni double silk satin lapels, turned-back cuffs and satin buttons.

This would be my choice to wear at a formal evening event.

Photographer: Stephen Hayward

opposite

SPRING/SUMMER COLLECTION 1993

Detail of tuxedo basque in ivory Hurel silk zibeline with black jet buttons over a fine sun-ray pleated skirt.

Vogue, July 1994: "Everything a Girl Needs for a Perfect Party."

Photographer: Paolo Roversi / The Condé Nast Publications Ltd.

AUTUMN/WINTER COLLECTION 1994/95

Halterneck dress in white silk Clerici georgette embroidered in silver bugle beads with crossover straps at the back and a deep slit at the centre front.

It was the drop-dead glamour of 1930s Hollywood that inspired this autumn's collection, and I included a range of halternecks, straps over bare backs, and slim columns embroidered in bugle beads in silvery white or jet black.

Photographer: Yoshie Nishikawa

opposite

AUTUMN/WINTER COLLECTION 1997/98

One-shouldered column with slanted hem in black Taroni heavy silk crepe.

This is a modern interpretation of the turn-of-the-century evening dress, whose skirts defined the hips and fell to a sweep at the hem like a lily. Here the fullness at the hem is removed but the sweep is retained, with a side slash and short train.

Photographer: Platon

Black jet dress in Clerici silk crepe.

Commissioned by HRH The Princess of Wales. "La Deuxieme nuit internationale de l'enfance" organised by UNESCO, December 1994.

The Princess was invited by Anne-Aymone Giscard d'Estaing on this official working visit in her capacity as president of Barnardo's Foundation for Children.

This was a special dress for me, as I am always very aware of the events in my home country and I was honoured that the Princess chose to wear one of my dresses at the Palace of Versailles. The Princess saw this dress on a visit to the studio one day and asked me to make it for this special occasion. It was our first "sexy" dress and, predictably, it received considerable coverage. Pierre Cardin commented "This is the home of the Sun King of France, now we have the Sun Princess of Versailles."

It was not long before this that the only dresses we worked on for the Princess were very formal. As I moved away from politically correct to slightly more sexy, I preserved the formality by still keeping them very structured inside.

This dress is draped towards the hip and held at an embroidered pocket. The inspiration for the embroidery originated from an antique picture frame which was finished with exquisite marquetry edged in "lead shot." I used black bugle beads for the marquetry and small boule for the lead-shot edging in the same proportion. I thought it made a pretty picture frame and here in the dress it frames the face and neck.

Photograph by REX Features

AUTUMN/WINTER COLLECTION 1996/97

Black Sfate & Combier crepe A-line shaped dress

In this dress, the sensuality of the back is focused by a jet asymmetric strap curving across it and along the hem.

Photographer: Yoshie Nishikawa

SPRING/SUMMER COLLECTION **1998**

White Clerici silk georgette long evening cruise dress with train and with a flock of white hand-embroidered chenille gulls.

The inspiration of this dress comes from a dress I designed for the Princess of Wales when she visited the Gulf States. The embroidered motif at that time was a falcon which we thought an appropriate symbol. The lightness of this almost transparent cruise dress contrasts with the formality of the Princess's state evening dress which was auctioned by Christie's in June 1997.

Photographer: Donna Francesca

Coatdress Redress

top right

AUTUMN/WINTER COLLECTION 1996/97

Brown wool Solbiati long jacket over shift dress.

Diana, Princess of Wales, with Ralph Lauren at a breakfast at the White House hosted by Hillary Clinton in aid of the Nina Hyde Centre for Breast Cancer Research, 24 September 1996.

All my collections include pinstripe jackets or coatdresses. Everyone looks taller and slimmer wearing them, and I love playing with the wide variety available. This wool pinstripe comes from Solbiati in Italy. The luxurious softness of the fabric lends itself to a softer shoulderline and a longer fluid jacket.

Photographer: Reuters/Stephen Jaffe/Archive Photos

bottom right

Diana, Princess of Wales, and Hillary Clinton.

Photograph by AP/Wide World Photos

opposite

AUTUMN/WINTER COLLECTION 1995/96

A-line trompe l'oeil coatdress in black and white pinstripe wool by Dormeuil with horn buttons.

I love the fluidity of the coatdress. This trompe l'oeil A-line version modernizes the coatdress shape by using traditionally masculine fabric.

Photographer: Platon

AUTUMN/WINTER
COLLECTION 1991/92

Double-breasted evening coatdress in Corisia wool pin-stripe with re-embroidered deep blue sequins and sapphire paste buttons.

HRH The Princess of Wales at Spencer House, November 1993.

The Princess visited her ancestral home, Spencer House, as a guest of honour marking the seventieth birthday of Henry Kissinger. The party had been organised by Lord Rothschild, Sir James Goldsmith, and Giovanni Agnelli. Lord Rothschild, who welcomed the Princess, had occupied Spencer House on a short lease and had done much work to restore it to its former glory.

The Princess liked this dress so much she didn't want to wait for one to be made, so I let her have this sample even though I had been photographed wearing it a little earlier myself at Vogue's seventy-fifth anniversary party.

Photograph by All Action

SPRING/SUMMER
COLLECTION 1998

Navy evening coatdress in Taroni heavy silk crepe with double silk duchess satin trimmings

In this collection I would add a touch of charm or flattery to otherwise very simple shapes. Here a peplum is constructed into a simply cut navy single-breasted tuxedo coatdress to lengthen the curve of the back.

Photographer: Stephen Hayward

Bands and Blazers

SPRING/SUMMER
COLLECTION 1989

Vogue, May 1989:
"Summer Breeze."

*This is an updated version of
a classic navy double-breasted
Dormeuil wool blazer that is cut
to elongate the body. It is worn
over a long-sleeved cotton jersey
scoop-neck top and cream
Corisia wool trousers.*

Photographer: Eddy Kohli / The Condé
Nast Publications Ltd.

above

SPRING/SUMMER COLLECTION 1991

Long-length Wain and Stewart wool blazer with coin buttons.

HRH The Princess of Wales granted a group of photographs to *Harper's Bazaar* to mark the occasion of her visit to the United States for the United Cerebral Palsy's Annual Awards Dinner, December 1995.

Having designed so many formal and correct clothes for the Princess I was delighted to make her this khaki blazer from the more casual part of my collection. Professionally this meant a lot to me, especially because she looks so wonderful and relaxed.

Photographer: Patrick Demarchelier

SPRING/SUMMER COLLECTION 1997

Navy Dormeuil wool gabardine blazer with nautical corded cuff in lieu of traditional button arrangement.

I called the summer 1997 collection "Summer in St. Petersburg." I found the mouldings of Russian architecture full of texture and interest, and this cuff detail was developed as three insets with piping from the elegant moulding of a column detail.

Photographer: Stephen Hayward

SPRING/SUMMER COLLECTION 1992

Inset jacket in navy Agnona and cream Garigue wool with pleated washed silk skirt with navy border.

TRH The Prince and Princess of Wales visited Liverpool Cathedral on 30 May 1993 for the fiftieth anniversary of the Battle of the Atlantic. The Princess chose this suit for its obvious nautical connotation. The jacket combines the tailoring of a blazer with the fluidity of a cardigan jacket. The skirt was a little too fluid for a windy May day in Liverpool.

Photographer: Tim Graham

opposite

Vogue, April 1992: "VIP Dressing: Suits with Social Graces, Matched with the Upwardly Mobile Hat."

Photographer: Terence Donovan / The Condé Nast Publications Ltd.
Spiral striped beret by Maison Michel,
Paris, for Catherine Walker

AUTUMN/WINTER
COLLECTION 1992/93

Black Abraham textured wool jacket.

HRH The Princess of Wales as Colonel-in-Chief of the Light Dragoons attends the annual dinner, November 1994.

Much of this collection was a play on how the tuxedo jacket could be given a military edge with various decorative treatments. This jacket has been appliquéed with satin ribbon to suggest military braiding. It is worn over a black skirt in Taroni double silk satin.

Photographer: Tim Graham

opposite

AUTUMN/WINTER
COLLECTION 1992/93

Inset basque in Taroni silk duchess satin and Buche silk velvet.

The longer basque shape is one of my favourites as it mirrors the formality of a jacket.

Photographer: Yoshie Nishikawa

Reds

above left

AUTUMN/WINTER COLLECTION 1995/96

Scarlet Riechers corded lace dress with Taroni double satin halterneck straps.

HRH The Princess of Wales on an official working visit to Buenos Aires, Argentina, November 1995.

The Princess attended a dinner in aid of the Association for Prevention of Infantile Paralysis at the Edificio Correo Centro (the Main Post Office) in a traffic-stopping red lace dress.

Photographer: Tim Rooke / REX Features

left

SPRING/SUMMER COLLECTION 1995

Lipstick red halterneck dress in Sfate & Combier crepe with Taroni double satin strap and buckle belt.

Vogue, May 1996: "Sweeping Understatement."

A red strapless column dress becomes a halterneck dress.

Photographer: Jacques Olivar / The Condé Nast Publications Ltd.

above

SPRING/SUMMER COLLECTION **1995**

Crepe shift dress with gold double buckle belt.

Diana, Princess of Wales, arriving to unveil a foundation stone at the casualty unit for children at Norwick Park Hospital, Harrow, July 1997.

I will always remember this simple shift dress and will always keep a replica in my archive. The Princess had ordered it a couple of years before wearing it here. It was her last daytime engagement.

Photograph by PA News

left

AUTUMN/WINTER COLLECTION **1997/98**

Red silk Clerici romain satin evening dress.

The drape of this dress becomes the back straps which continue from the back around the low waist as a belt.

Photographer: Stephen Hayward

AUTUMN/WINTER
COLLECTION 1996/97

Red Clerici silk crepe drap halterneck dress with high slit and small train.

Tatler, September 1995: "Here's looking at you, Kidd."

Jodie Kidd wears this simple sexy evening dress which just had to be made in red.

Photographer: J. R. Duran / The Condé Nast Publications Ltd.

opposite

AUTUMN/WINTER
COLLECTION 1997/98

Valentine red rose bustier dress in Clerici silk satin with spiralling rose climbing to a strap.

This collection drew on the romanticism of Russian folk-lore. This particular piece was inspired by a beautifully ornate hand-embroidered shawl which, when thrown over the shoulders, gave this sinuous spiralling effect of roses around the body. These roses are handmade and embroidered onto the dress in matching tone-on-tone colours.

Photographer: Platon

Cords and Stitches

AUTUMN/WINTER
COLLECTION **1996/97**

**Polo-neck dress in navy Buche silk
velvet and Taroni single silk satin.**

*This A-line sleeveless shift with its multiple
rows of neck piping is a modern interpretation of the high-necked Edwardian blouse.*

Photographer: Platon

opposite

SPRING/SUMMER COLLECTION **1997**

**Palest blue bias-cut Taroni silk crepe
evening dress with graduated chevron
details in stone silk duchess satin.**

*The coolness and ease of this bias-cut, shoe-
string dress are complemented by the softness
of the ice blue and beige colouring and the
lightness of construction. This is a minimalist
dress, which is shown here to illustrate the
younger couture of my later collections.*

Photographer: Platon

AUTUMN/WINTER COLLECTION 1994/95

Halterneck dress in navy Buche silk drap and Taroni silk satin duchess cording.

HRH The Princess of Wales with Liz Tilberis at the Council for Fashion Designers of America Gala, New York, February 1995.

Liz's enthusiasm for life is infectious and I am grateful for the support she gave me as editor of British Vogue. *In a piece written as a tribute to the Princess in* Harper's Bazaar, *Liz wrote "when she got out of the car at Lincoln Center, looking unbelievably beautiful in a blue strappy Catherine Walker gown with her hair slicked back, the 'been there, done that' New York fashion crowd stopped dead in their tracks."*

Photographers: Dave Chancellor / Alpha, REX Features

AUTUMN/WINTER COLLECTION 1996/97

Midnight blue Riechers lace evening dress with loose petticoat hem and deep corded back.

Diana, Princess of Wales, at the film premiere of *In Love and War* in support of the work of the Red Cross in Angola, February 1997.

The Princess chose this dress for this film premiere because of its simple silhouette with satin cording framing the face. I have used Riechers lace for nearly twenty years. It has a beautiful "handle" and I love the gentle poetry of the designs. I am also a little biased because it is manufactured in Marck, which is not far from where I spent part of my childhood in Northern France.

Photographers: PA News (left), Brendan Beirne / REX Features (right)

SPRING/SUMMER
COLLECTION 1998

Navy and ivory Taroni silk georgette long evening dress with train, with hand-embroidered chenille carnations trailing across the body.

Hand embroidering the velvety chenille onto georgette creates the sensuality of devore in reverse which is fresher for the summer.

Photographer: Donna Francesca

opposite

SPRING/SUMMER
COLLECTION 1998

Navy Clerici silk georgette long evening dress with hand-embroidered chenille rope design.

The sinuous line of this sheath cruise dress is accentuated by the stark white chenille rope embroidery that flows down to the line of the bias-cut train.

Photographer: Donna Francesca

left and opposite

AUTUMN/WINTER COLLECTION 1997/98

Royal blue Buche silk velvet trained column dress with spiralling stitchwork roses.

The "ton-sur-ton" stitchwork was a favourite of the dressmakers of the belle époque. *In those days the stitchwork was undertaken by hand whereas this embroidery is produced on a traditional embroidery machine (mysteriously known in the embroidery world as "The Irish Machine"). The embroiderer guides the work by hand, and although there is a basic pattern, it is to some extent freehand.*

Photographer: Stephen Hayward

left

AUTUMN/WINTER COLLECTION 1997/98

Black Buche silk velvet embroidered bustier dress with slanting hem.

In this dress, the upward slant and punctuation of the embroidery emphasises the slimness of the silhouette. The slanting hem also accentuates the train and shows the leg from the knee.

Photographer: Stephen Hayward

Laces

Black Riechers lace dress and veil.

Commissioned by HRH The Princess of Wales.
Papal Audience, Rome, April 1985.

This was an occasion where the Princess's visual impact clearly needed to be different from that of her usual appointments, and so when I received this commission I had to resist trying to make a "fashion statement."

I visited the Vatican in March and interviewed one or two Vatican officials as part of my research. I was also able to visit the Vatican library to see how others had addressed the similar assignments. This was not very helpful, and all I could find was a picture of Sophia Loren and the Queen of Spain as precedents, both with a quite different approach to dress! I did however find some guidelines and in a way the design was derived more from what was not acceptable than from any positive direction: Only Catholic queens were allowed to wear a colour other than black; there were certain rules on what parts of the body should be covered; and of course a mantilla was required.

I chose a dress rather than a suit because it was softer and more modest than my usual tailoring, which was generally close fitting. The Princess had had a navy velvet dress with lace inset from my last collection which she loved and found very comfortable, and so I used a similar shape here.

The lace is finely corded over a black silk bodice with long sleeves and Elizabethan collar. A mid-calf length seemed younger than full length and the scalloped hem lightened the all-black image.

Photographer: Ron Bell / PA News

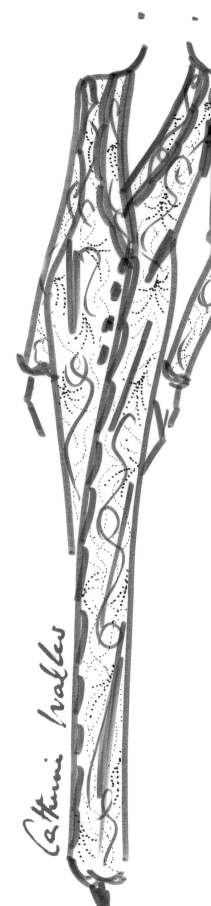

Catherine Walker

Grand coatdress in white Riechers lace with ice blue and white sequin and embroidery.

Commissioned by HRH The Princess of Wales for a state visit to France and worn at a dinner hosted by French Minister of Culture Jacques Lang, Château de Chambord, November 1988.

I chose white lace for this commission because it was a textile common at the court of Versailles, but I tailored it into a modern shape. Given the Princess's sense of panache I really do not know anyone else who could carry off this long sheath of glittering icy embroidery in quite the way she did.

This reception was also attended by HRH Princess Caroline of Monaco, and there was tremendous press interest in what the Princesses would wear on this occasion. HRH Princess Caroline of Monaco was dressed by the House of Dior.

Photographer: Tim Graham

below

HRH The Princess of Wales with HRH Princess Caroline of Monaco.

Photograph by Camera Press

AUTUMN/WINTER COLLECTION 1996/97

Pearl, sequin, and crystal embroidered Riechers lace dress.

Diana, Princess of Wales, with Anna Wintour and Ralph Lauren at the fund-raising gala for the Nina Hyde Centre for Breast Cancer Research, Washington D.C., September 1996.

During the two seasons of autumn 1995 and spring 1996 my work with the Princess slowed down while I was recovering from breast cancer. I was in better shape by the autumn of 1996, and this was the first major dress we worked on after my illness, so it has strong emotional meaning for me. It was also an important occasion for the Princess, and I know she had to summon her courage for this first major engagement after her divorce.

This embroidery was designed to emulate the subtlety of antique pearls. The English "flattery" is encapsulated through the shades of white tinged with pale blue, pink, and ivory. This embroidery was a derivative of earlier work we had done together for a state dress (see page 144) that she loved for its old-fashioned mother-of-pearl gleam and sheer regal charm.

During her speech in Washington the Princess quoted the Australian poet Adam Lindsay Gordon:

Life is mostly froth and bubble
Two things stand like stone
Kindness in another's trouble
Courage in your own.

After the Princess returned to London she sent me a short note that I was thrilled to receive. She wrote, "It's impossible to put into words the thrill of wearing such a beautiful dress as your cream lace one! I was so proud and felt very confident to stride out there and deliver my first speech since the divorce . . . The comments about your design and expertise would have made your ears burn. You gave an enormous amount of people an enormous amount of pleasure . . . Thank you.".

Photographer: Tim Rooke /
REX Features

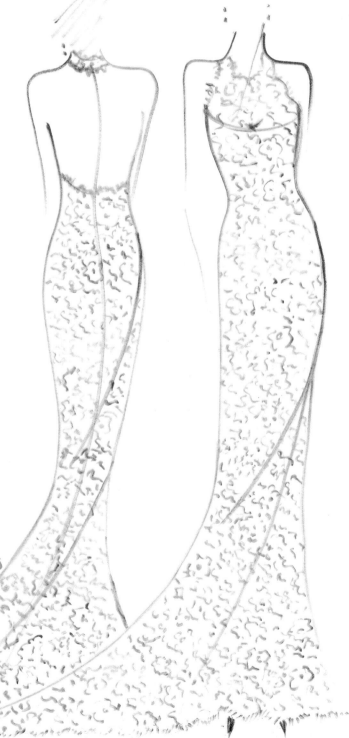

Diamanté lace cap-sleeve cream silk embroidered shift dress.

Commissioned by HRH The Princess of Wales in November 1990 for an official visit to Pakistan in January 1991.

Although this is a very modest shift dress I chose to embroider it with a richly encrusted Mogul "tapestry"-inspired design using gold and silver bugle beads and sequins.

The dress was worn in public for the first time during a working visit to Moscow at the Bolshoi ballet where its slightly Byzantine appearance was also appropriate. It is seen here when the Princess visited the London Coliseum in March 1996 as patron of the English National Ballet for the ballet version of Alice in Wonderland.

Photographer: Richard Gillard / Camera Press

opposite

State dinner dress (detail).

Commissioned by HRH The Princess of Wales for a diplomatic reception at Buckingham Palace, November 1993.

The Princess asked me to design this dress when she and Prince Charles were about to announce their separation. Her brief to me was to design a banquet dress in a very grand and formal style. I chose this formal duchess silk satin by Hurel, gathered it at the waist and softened it with a traditional lace bodice in a buttermilk shade gently picked out in pearls, crystals, and mother-of-pearl sequins. The dress was not seen in public until it was photographed as an official portrait by Lord Snowdon in 1997.

Photographer: Stephen Hayward

Ice blue Taroni silk crepe shift dress with "ice rose" embroidery.

Commissioned by Diana, Princess of Wales, in April 1997, for the Christie's gala evening, London, to support the auction of the dresses belonging to Diana, Princess of Wales, 2 June 1997.

For sixteen years of dressing the Princess I had kept a low profile and was only photographed with her once (on the steps of Hereford Cathedral in 1988). However, the Princess had urged me to "step out" for this auction which was obviously going to raise substantial donations to her charities. She knew how important this was for me, too, as this was my first public event since my illness with cancer in 1995. I had received unfailing support from the Princess during my illness and I was delighted to know that my designs, through the Princess's charitable work, were now to be used to save lives.

Photographer: Tim Graham

opposite

SPRING/SUMMER COLLECTION 1995/96

Embroidered halterneck dress with a draped skirt in pale blue Taroni silk georgette.

I always try to give my embroidery a three-dimensional quality not only by tilting the image in perspective but also with the texture itself. Here the bugle beads and diamanté are so dense that they rise from the surface of the fabric like florets made of sugar.

Photographer: Stephen Hayward

SPRING/SUMMER COLLECTION 1997

Edwardian-style slip dress in dove grey Buche silk georgette with graduated sequins and beaded embroidery.

The softness of the mid-1990s is emphasized in the pale embroidery of this collection dress. The construction of the dress is lighter and the colourway is delicately shaded to reflect the more simple shape.

Photographer: Platon

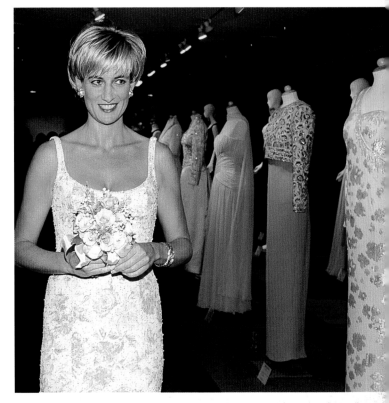

Glass-beaded floral slip dress.

Commissioned by Diana, Princess of Wales,
for the Christie's Auction Gala, New York,
23 June 1997.

*This dress was embroidered in iridescent sequins
and clear crystal to mirror the pale grey and cream
tones of one of our own fabric prints from the Russian collection this season.*

*Although the Princess chose to wear two similar
simple embroidered shifts in London and New
York for the receptions preceding the auction of
her dresses, she wanted to convey a very different
feeling in each case and the embroidery and fabrics
were quite different. In London, the ice-blue fabric
with its rich ice-rose embroidery seemed appropriate, but for New York we wanted the embroidery
to be lighter and more understated in this calm,
neutral print.*

Photographer: Tim Graham

SPRING/SUMMER COLLECTION 1993

Draped column dress in dove grey silk Taroni georgette with bustier embroidered in a "French needlepoint lace" pattern.

The design of the bustier embroidery is based on the work of Anna Maria Garthwaite, an eighteenth-century artist whose beautiful drawings for woven silk are available for study at the Victoria and Albert Museum in London.

Photographer: Stephen Hayward

opposite

SPRING/SUMMER COLLECTION 1993

Detail of long embroidered basque in Buche silk georgette over fine sun-ray pleated skirt

In this collection I used the beauty of French needlepoint lace as an inspiration for much of the embroidery. This dress was based on a portrait of Maria Isabella de Bourbon by Nattier. The strapless basque is embroidered in the palest pink graduated pearls.

Photographer: Stephen Hayward

SPRING/SUMMER
COLLECTION 1993

Vogue, May 1995: "Sweet Dreams.
The Pink of Perfection: balletic
grace is summoned up in yard
upon yard of soft tulle and a richly
beaded bodice."

Photographer: Nick Knight / The Condé
Nast Publications Ltd.
Model: Amber Valletta

Acknowledgments

My thanks in the preparation of this book go to:

Tamasin Day-Lewis
Christine Harrison

for their help in researching and writing

Patrick Demarchelier
Donna Francesca
Tim Graham
Stephen Hayward
Yoshie Nishikawa
Platon
Geoff Wilkinson

for their original photography

Paul Burrell

for his kind advice

Universe Publishing

for their guidance and patience